"One of the most beautiful, touching stories I've

**- JERRY BONKOWSKI,** Award-winning writer for NASCAR Talk and MotorSports Talk - NBC Sports and co-host of NASCAR

"A human interest story times ten."

**- PAT GALVIN,** Drag Racing Veteran

"Top Fuel for Life is the first book of its kind. You don't see books about happiness authored by a man's man. Jim O Oberhofer's honest story about pain and love is transformative. Be prepared to walk away with eyes wide open after reading his story. I wish I had this book when I first started out in life!"

**- SCOTT GARWOOD,** Cofounder of Transformational Growth Partners

"Jim O's path to happiness is both remarkable and inspiring. His honest, funny and poignant storytelling gives us all hope that we can get through anything in life-as long as we believe in love."

**- JACKIE CAMACHO-RUIZ,** International speaker and seven-time author, including *The Fig Factor*

"Life, in many ways, can be just like a dragster going 300+ mph. In order to have the best experience, you have to be aware of what is happening around you and react to those things right up until you reach the finish line. Life, like drag racing, challenges us whether we are ready or not. Jim O's book is for everyone who wants to learn about becoming stronger and finding happiness after losing the most important person in their life. *Top Fuel For Life* shows how important it is to find happiness and appreciation in the day-to-day of living."

**- BRETT SHAW,** *President of Mac Tools*

JIM OBERHOFER

# TOP FUEL FOR LIFE

LIFE LESSONS FROM A
CREW CHIEF

# Top Fuel For Life

Cover and layout design: Juan Pablo Ruiz.

Printed in the United States of America

ISBN: 978-1939794-05-5

# Contents:

When you take a long hard look at your life,
I guarantee you that being a winner has little to
do with crossing the finish line first. After many
mistakes and a whole lot of heartache, I learned
that happiness comes from a deeper, simpler place.
That's the big win.

**– Jim O**

# PROLOGUE: A LOVE LETTER

*Dear Tammy,*

*I miss you and I love you! Those are the first words that come to mind when I think of you, and I think of you every day. A lot has been going on since you left us on June 18, 2013. One thing that I know you would be proud of is how well Ashley is doing. She is truly an amazing young lady and we all know you are the reason she is. It's hard to believe that she is twenty years old now . . . how time flies!*

*Ashley also has a boyfriend. His name is Isaac and he is a good kid, and better yet . . . he's very good to Ashley. Do you remember the calendars you would fill out with everyone's birthday from all the teams on them? Well, in 2013, one of the only birthdays you filled out in that calendar was Isaac's . . . and Ashley noticed that and took it as a sign from you. Isaac works on the DHL Funny Car, so not only is his girlfriend's dad his boss, but so is his girlfriend's uncle, and Jon O lets him know that. This poor kid gets more grief from everyone at the shop, but he handles it very well. I know you would have loved him and his family . . . especially since they are from Maine. They've been going out now for over two years, and I don't see that changing any time soon.*

*It's funny how every time Ashley talks, she reminds so many people of you. She has so many of your good qualities. I am very proud of her and very blessed that she is our daughter . . . you did such an amazing job raising her!*

*You're probably also wondering about Tex the cat. Well, he has been doing good, and I'm pretty sure he has used up almost all of his nine lives. Ashley just calls him "Cat" now, and he is quite entertaining. I know that he misses you because every now and then you can tell he is looking for you. He is a good cat and Ashley just loves him like crazy.*

*Your mom and dad seem to be doing well. I don't talk to them as much as I should, and for that I apologize. The same goes for your brother Tim. I just need to get better about making time to give them a call or just take a trip to Ohio. I always try to remind Ashley to give them a call, but I'm not sure how often she does that. Your sister Teri and I text each other a lot. She always wishes us good luck every race day morning, which is always nice. Her and Bubba always come out to the Houston and Dallas races, and, as usual , Teri does all the talking and Bubba is just as laid back as ever. Can you believe your nephew Ryan graduated from high school this year? I couldn't believe it when I got the announcement. I know you would have said the same thing I said: "Wasn't he just born the other day?" Before you know it, Jared will be next!*

*Your Kalitta team has been doing well the last couple of years, and I think you would be proud. Doug finally got that Wally for you that you so wanted at Dallas in 2013, and he's picked up four more since then. Alexis won her first race at Phoenix in 2014, and then won Indy later that year! Both Alexis and Del won at your favorite place, Las Vegas, as it was a Team Kalitta Funny Car sweep in Sin City in 2014!*

*I know one thing that would have bothered you is the change* we made with Connie's car early last year. Connie decided that he wanted to make a driver change in his car so he replaced Grubby with JR Todd. I know how much you loved Grubby and it was a difficult time for everyone, but somehow it all worked out. JR has been a great addition to the team, and I know you would have loved him too! He won the Denver race and finished second in the points in 2014. Grubby is now a crew chief for Clay Millican and is doing a great job. I guess all things happen for a reason, even though we sometimes never know what that reason is.

Speaking of Connie . . . he's doing good and hasn't changed a bit! Well, he did get a knee replacement finally, and I think that is going to help him live another fifty years! The man never stops moving forward, which I think keeps him young. He just keeps buying and flying airplanes and looks for ways to make his race cars go quick and fast. I know how much you loved Connie and cared for him, and I know he felt the same way about you! He is an amazing guy and I could never thank him enough for everything he has done for our family. The whole Kalitta family is just flat-out awesome!

Rachel and Tommy D got married down in Cancun earlier this year and both Ashley and I went and had a great time. Chrissy and Shawn are doing a great job in the office making sure all of the crew guys turn in their receipts. I think it's going better because Chrissy threatened them all with bodily harm. Patricia finally got that picnic table you always wanted out in front of the Kalitta offices. When the weather is nice I always see Patricia and Sarah having lunch out there. Megan moved on to the University of Michigan where she is taking nursing classes and working in the hospital. She is also getting *married on October 10, and Ashley and I will be there.*

*Cowboy Bob has been awesome as usual. It's hard to say where I would be without him. He has helped keep me on the right path, even when I tend to veer off path as I often do. I am truly lucky to have him in my life . . . he is the big brother I never had!*

*My side of the family has been doing well. My mom and dad are the same as usual, and my brother and Kim are doing well. Jess and Julia keep getting older and prettier every day, which is going to give Jon O way more gray hair than me! My sister moved out to Vegas and is now working for Cowboy Bob.*

*Me . . . I've been doing OK. I struggle from time to time, missing you and trying to figure out where my life is going these days, but all in all it's been pretty good and our daughter is the reason for that. I think the overwhelming support that Ashley and I received from the drag racing community kept both of us moving forward, and for that, I am truly grateful! The drag racing community is such a strong group, and it showed. It was so cool that everyone wanted to display one of the decals we made for you on their race cars! It just showed how much you were loved.*

*One thing that we did after your passing was adopt a panda in your name from Pandas International out of Denver. With the help of Jesse James and all of the people who bought the "777" wristbands that Jesse had made and sold at the race track, we were able to raise enough money to adopt a panda! The name of the panda is Tammy Sue and she has a birthday in August just like you! Tammy Sue lives in China and loves sleeping and eating bamboo. We can even watch Tammy Sue on a live TV feed that they have over in China. I know your sister enjoys that. People can say whatever they want about Jesse, but both you and I know that he has a big heart and is a very good guy!*

*It's hard to imagine that three of your birthdays . . . two of our wedding anniversaries . . . two Christmas's and two New Year's, two Valentine's Days and two Mother's Days have gone by since you've been gone. Every time we get closer to one of these days, I think of you even more—if that's possible! I always wish you were here to talk to, to hold and to love!. That old saying of "you don't know what you have until it's gone" . . . well, that saying is so true!*

*I never did get to tell you how proud I was of you with how you fought cancer. You were truly stronger than anybody I ever knew. If I had one percent of the courage that you did, I would be that much better of a person than I am now. I know that I love to talk about you with people and about how hard you fought. For some reason it makes me feel good to talk about you and how courageous you were with your fight against cancer.*

*It's probably hard to believe that I'm writing a book! I know when the idea was first presented to me, I just laughed. How could someone like me write a book when I get corrected by Ashley on a daily basis about spelling and punctuation? She definitely takes after you with proper spelling and punctuation, and still finds typos everywhere she can.*

*I guess my main motivation for writing this book was to let people know how I failed in so many ways with you in understanding your illness. I wanted to let people know how lucky I was to have you as my wife and have Ashley as our daughter. I wanted to let people know that happiness doesn't always come from winning races or championships. Sometimes it comes from the simplest things—like ice cream.*

*I really hope that this book helps people who may be struggling with an illness, with a marriage or maybe just life in general, to know that simple happiness is easily achieved and is more important than anything in this world.*

*I also wanted to start something that you would be proud of. I know how much you loved and cared about kids, and with that I want to start a charity that helps get disabled or less fortunate kids out to the drag races. My dream is to have kids at every race we go to and have them be part of the Kalitta team. I want to start the Tammy O Foundation with the proceeds from this book and try and make a difference.*

*I know you're up in heaven and I hope that you are playing bingo with your Grandma Matoski and my Grandma Hovenac. I hope there is a big casino up there with slot machines that come up winners every time. I hope there are pandas all over the place and that you and Scott drink Coors Light every day. Most of all, I hope you know that I loved you and continue to love you and miss you every day.*

*Someday I will see you again, so save me a seat!*

*I love you!*


*Love,*

**Jim O**

*October 2015*

**P.S.** *If you haven't already figured it out, the words on these pages are dedicated to you, Tammy O.*

# PART ONE:

# LIES

# THE GREEN DRESS

*A Top Fuel car can drive the length of a football field in one second. And that's about all it takes to fall in love.*

There's a certain sound, a music you hear on a shop floor. It was playing the day I first saw Tammy Sue Ferrell. Firecracker sparks jumped from a welder and sizzled like my mom's crackling bacon on a Sunday morning. Tools fell hard on the gray concrete floor sending out trios of high-pitched clink, clink, clinks. The steady hummmmmmm of an air compressor rounded out the orchestra echoing off cinder block walls. Somewhere, people were cracking jokes. Billy Joel belted out "We Didn't Start the Fire." You see, there just aren't any good acoustics in a 25,000-square-foot airplane hangar, and that's where our race cars lived back in late 1989 at Kalitta Motorsports in Ypsilanti, Michigan. Sound bounced around like atoms in one of those boring science movies I slept through in grade school.

Wearing a faded T-shirt and frayed jeans covered in grit, a leaner, younger version of myself prepped a new Funny Car body for paint. I had finished a section, the dust settling in my ears and hair when I set down the sander. I looked up. I could hear her soft sweet voice before I actually saw the woman walking alongside driver Scott Kalitta, the man whose car I was getting ready to paint. She laughed at something Scott said. She wore a green sleeveless dress just above the knee. High heels, short hair, pretty. There was something about the way she moved. She was going to be our new public relations girl. That was the first time I saw her, the woman I would fall in love with and marry two and a half years later in a souped-up Las Vegas chapel.

Of course, Scott told me to stay away from Tammy and that she was Tim Ferrell's younger sister. Like working with this former Kalitta guy (he had moved on to become a crew chief for Top Fuel driver Earl Whiting) gave Scott ownership of the man's sister for crying out loud. I'd known Tim for about five years before meeting Tammy, too . . . so what? I didn't listen to Scott's hemming and hawing. I ignored it all. Tammy's smile filled her eyes with light. I liked that.

Here are three things I can tell you about my life: I had it all. I didn't know it until it was almost too late. And then it was gone.

I don't want regret to burn you. That's why I'm passionate about sharing my story. Learn from my mistakes. If this book opens the door to a better life for you and you alone, then I've done something good. I've accomplished something big.

This is the true story of how I found happiness—that messy, crowded, sacred place where we find ourselves smack in the middle of the people we love and our worst day is never really that bad because life is full and that fullness cushions our falls. We have everything we need, everything we want. If life has a greater purpose, it's to be happy. Took me a long time to understand happiness. I'm not talking about the high that comes from collecting trophies and being a famous guy in the infamous Kalitta mosh pit where we all gather on the track, swinging fists after a big win. Because guess what? That moment lasts a few minutes and then it's over. I'm talking about the deeper, forever happiness of relationships, love, friendship and honest living. The salty kind of happiness you taste when you kiss someone you love on an open beach or when you throw back popcorn watching a movie with your family and everybody's in their pajamas. Or when you laugh hard over beers with the neighbors in the driveway after mowing the grass. This kind of happiness is never plugged into your calendar. It's the kind that is just there for the taking. Like when your husband says he loves you. Or your wife plans an evening out. And these special moments happen on a Tuesday. After three kids and two decades of marriage. And it's not your anniversary.

That's the happiness I'm talking about.

Let's put it this way, if the thrill from a Kalitta mosh pit symbolizes the feeling of winning big, then why not feel that way about your life? Let's take the daily grind, the unexpected detours, the challenges with our kids and our marriages and our jobs and celebrate all of it—good or bad—with one big, whooping, victory mosh pit (with less bruises, of course) every day. It took losing someone I loved for me to discover this all-in kind of happiness. In time, I'll show you exactly where I found it. I promise.

# LITTLE RED DRAGSTER

*In 1959, the NHRA mandated the parachute-braking system whereby large, billowy parachutes reverse the force of high-speed dragsters. Similarly, it's amazing how holding back emotion slows us down until, one day, we find it easier to "do" life rather than "feel" life.*

I'm a crew chief for the Mac Tools Top Fuel dragster driven by Doug Kalitta. In between races, I carry around business cards that say "Jim O Oberhofer, Vice President of Operations, Kalitta Motorsports." I shuffle a lot of papers (that's what some people think) in order to keep sponsors, inventory and business moving forward for four teams: two Top Fuel dragsters and two Funny Cars.

You might be familiar with NASCAR or Formula One racing. Well let me tell you, the earth-shattering sound, the flames and the desire for a driver to dominate the track is just as exciting in Top Fuel or Funny Car.

A Top Fuel car looks like a long pencil with small wheels at its tip and big wheels at the part where you'd find the eraser. They are the quickest cars on earth, like land-based missiles. With an estimated 10,000-horsepower engine, they use nitromethane for fuel to reach up to 330 mph from a standing start in about 3.7 seconds, along a straight 1,000-foot track. Funny Cars are the next class down from Top Fuel with a carbon fiber body that mimics a car you might see on the street, and with a much shorter wheelbase than the Top Fuel car. They reach about 320 mph in

4.00 seconds on that same 1,000-foot track.

I imagined myself in racing since I was a kid.

My younger brother Jon O and I rode Big Wheels with parachutes made out of big black plastic garbage bags to catch the wind in the back. We rigged them to crash down the hilly streets around our house in Saddle Brook, New Jersey, as we sailed down Dewey Avenue, the street we lived on. Our sound effects were awful and loud as we revved the engines of our "Top Fuel" cars. We laughed our heads off when the yellow and orange Big Wheel parts exploded across the pavement. (People always said he and I look a lot alike—we both have thick, dark brown hair, blue eyes and aren't real tall and aren't real short. The big difference is that Jon O has no butt. He got that feature from my dad.)

Let me explain the "O" thing, just to get it out of the way. It goes back to when I was a kid. My dad is Dave O, a tall guy, about six feet two inches tall, and back when we were kids, he had thick black wavy hair and a silent, almost brooding look you'd expect to see on James Dean. I'm told he was a good-looking guy, but I just always thought I was in trouble the way he'd tilt his head down slightly, his eyes demanding answers while my mind retraced my steps. My mom was Sue O, the most beautiful woman on earth. Tall and slender with dark blond hair, Mom was always smiling; she made every bad situation better by just being there—she was always in a good mood. I mean she had a better happiness record than a fairy godmother. My sister is Suzie O, and my brother and I usually just tolerated her. She always seemed like too much trouble to us back then, but we would always take care of her no matter how much of a pain in the ass we thought she was. We kids inherited the O without question. Some parents hand down pictures, mine gave us a letter. And yes, I'm passing it down too. Just ask my daughter Ashley O.

A little more than four decades have gone by since the Big Wheel days. Conrad "The Bounty Hunter" Kalitta, long time boss-mentor-pain-in-the-neck-and-father-figure to me, once told me that looking at your rear view mirror means you're not going forward. Connie is a self-made legend who, unlike a lot of racers of his caliber, does not relive the glory days or fawn over old cars. He has more history than anyone I know, yet, he never dwells on it. He focuses only on the "now."

Sometimes, though, you have to look back to see what went wrong. You have to look back in order to fix yourself.

And I was, for more years than I would like to say, broken.

***

From the time I can remember, my dad ran a paint and body shop. He painted East Coast race cars: wild-colored Funny Cars, sleek dragsters and anything else that would blast down a dragstrip. These bodies were built to beat the wind.

Dad would take Jon O and me to races put on by the National Hot Rod Association. Like Major League Baseball oversees baseball, the NHRA manages the sport of drag racing. They make the rules and organize the twenty-four races that make up our season from February to November. We were in love with the coolest sport on earth. We were born to be race car drivers, or so we thought. Our friends at school envied our T-shirts with designs of sleek cars. Our stories about the drag races made the lunch table circuit.

Mrs. Maddaroshian, my second grade teacher, wasn't impressed. In her mid-thirties with shoulder-length dark hair always combed smooth, she took her profession seriously and her students to heart from Franklin Elementary School. She was greatly concerned the day she called my mother in.

"The assignment each day," she said flatly, as her tan hands straightened out the papers on her desk, "is to draw a picture using a different color. Mrs. Oberhofer, every day Jim draws a dragster."

Sure enough, Monday's car was red, Tuesday's car was yellow, Wednesday's car was purple and so on. Mrs. Maddaroshian spread out the papers in front of my mother like they were key evidence in a murder trial. She and I both sat in chairs off to the side of my teacher's big desk. Mom looked down at the papers. Very professional, wearing a nice blouse and a short straight skirt, my mother politely explained my dad's job painting cars, especially race cars, and the fact that he also drag raced. She said she would talk to me about expanding my . . . what did she call it . . . repertoire. My teacher nodded, accepting that justice had been served (although probably not as much as she would have liked). After meeting with Mrs. Maddaroshian, we walked out, my mother's arm around my shoulder. She looked down at me, her eyebrows raised and her voice as firm yet soft as Texas sheet cake, "Jim O, you're not in trouble, but can you draw something else besides a dragster tomorrow in school?"

My mom was born into happiness. Grandpa Hovenac was always smiling—even after he lost his hair at an early age. He designed Christmas cards for American Telephone & Telegraph Co. and painted pictures for all of us in the family. Grandma Hovenac, just so you know, thought I could do no wrong. She was the poster child for grandmas. To this day, I carry in my backpack the small, shiny gold angel pins she gave me as a child. "Now, Jimmy, you take these pins and the angels will protect you. Close your eyes and pray, Jimmy, pray the angels keep you safe." *OK, Grandma*, I would say. We could have burned their house down with a random match, and they still would have loved us!

One of Grandma Hovenac's proudest moments of all time was my First Holy Communion, a Catholic sacrament we receive in order to take the Holy Eucharist at Sunday Mass. All of us guys dressed in suits and the girls wore pretty white dresses and veils as we paraded, palms together, into St. Leo's Church. I liked wearing a tie. It made me feel grown up. On that day, my mom was smiling even wider than usual—if that's even possible.

While my mom influenced my faith, my dad oversaw how I spent my time and that meant that, while other kids were whittling bears out of bars of soap during Cub Scout meetings and having sleepovers, Jon O and I were hanging along the fence at the track like laundry on a summer clothesline, happily eating the dust of the fastest cars on earth. It was there that we got the breath knocked out of our lungs. I can still remember the smell of burning rubber mixed with nitromethane and lots of noise . . . I could hear the engines through my feet, through my whole body. The vibrations ran through us like a jackhammer cutting through concrete, our hearts racing, our hands covering our ears, splinters of black rubber kicking up into the stands. In between races, we were regulars at the concession stand, feeling like big shots ordering our own hamburgers and hot dogs, enjoying the freedom of not being under my dad's watchful eye.

Back in the sixties, my dad had driven and tuned a junior fuel dragster with a passion for speed he would hand down to Jon O and me. He took that love of racing with him after he married my mom. From the time I was in kindergarten until around fourth grade, Dad and his partners Frank Johdus and Jim Grace, who was the driver, had a Top Fuel car called the Pleasure Seekers. The idea behind the name was simple: The group wanted to show how they got pleasure by (hopefully) beating the bigger names in drag racing. Top Fuel racing was in its heyday, trumping every race car known to man in speed and sound. It did not, however, feed a family.

My dad had us kids to take care of—but racing was in his blood. There were bills to pay—but the boys at the track were waiting for him. He didn't want us living paycheck to paycheck—but, screw it, there were races he could win. Yep, that car pulled at him all right, in two different directions. He just couldn't take it the distance. It was a familiar road. He tried to serve our country, but the military rejected him because he had bad feet. He wanted to buy us a house, but all we could afford was a four-room apartment in Jersey.

Of course, I was a kid. I couldn't figure out why adults didn't eat ice cream all day long. So I really, really couldn't understand why he didn't just work on the car whenever he wanted to. I mean the wheels were sitting right there. I was too young to understand that racing is an expensive sport. It wasn't easy making money painting cars, especially on the East Coast. Besides, I had my own "career" going as a pitcher and third baseman. We even clinched the Little League championship one year. I've still got the trophy in my basement. I loved when our team won. That big win was the first time I felt like I had done something really important in my life, and I didn't do it alone. It was all of us, the whole team.

After the Pleasure Seekers dragster ran off the end of the National Trail Raceway near Hebron, Ohio, the car was finished. My dad then teamed up with Hank Endres, Chip Brown and Bill Clark on the Nirvana Top Fuel dragster for the 1976 and '77 racing seasons. Hank sat in the cockpit of the car carefully put together by my dad and his new partners. During race weekends, all four of them would tune and work on the Nirvana dragster. It was a much different racing world back then. The financial pressure to keep cars running, however, always has been part of the sport.

As a father now, what came next makes sense: My dad wanted a better life for us and that better life turned out to be almost sixteen hundred miles away in Plano, Texas. I was ten years old. The cost of living was less, there was no state income tax, and he could finally afford to buy us a house. He had been dreaming of us settling down in the land of ten-gallon hats and country music after going to a race there back in the early seventies.

The last thing I remember before leaving Jersey was my mom trying to keep us three kids in line and fed while my dad packed up our apartment with a steady energy that didn't stop until the last box was taped. Our family shuffled out the apartment door one last time, bags, boxes and suitcases in hand.

We tumbled into the family's 1977 brown, four-door Chevy Silverado pickup truck, with an overloaded U-Haul trailer on the hitch, that my mom drove. My dad drove a Hertz rental truck that had every stick of furniture we owned and tools and equipment from his shop. I'm pretty sure the belly of the truck skimmed the road now and then. My mom was silent and focused, checking to make sure she had everything she needed to keep us kids entertained, but still giving us that million dollar smile to make us all feel like moving across country was old hat.

Our family of five set out for the Lone Star State. It was November 1977. I wasn't happy, Jon O didn't care, and my baby sister Suzie complained the WHOLE, STINKIN' WAY TO TEXAS about leaving her friends. When that racing season ended, so did my dad's Top Fuel career. With every mile west, he left behind his passion for racing, his parents and in-laws, and all our extended family so us kids would have a future.

One thing we all came to understand very quickly was that our world had changed. We'd traded a bustling, urban environment and all our relatives back home for an endless expanse of hot, dry earth.

Plano was spread out and somewhat slower in pace. The school was a lot bigger than the one in Saddle Brook and, in my young mind, "choppy." Pick an age group and they had a school for it: kindergarten to fifth, middle school for sixth to eighth, high school for ninth and tenth grade, and senior high school for eleventh and twelfth. I missed all the cousins we used to get in trouble with at family dinners. Texans like to say with great pride that everything in their state is "bigger." Well, it sure was bigger than where we came from. But my dad liked the place and, more importantly, he wanted to give us a better life. Texas was a clean start.

Did my dad ever look back? I've never asked him. Walking in his shoes as a father now, I think I know what he would have said: When you have children, your heart doesn't belong to you anymore. There's no room for "I want." He gave up his comfort zone. It took a lot of courage to leave his parents and siblings, his hometown. We could have just kept going; it's easy to keep doing what you always know. Hell, how many times in life do we stay in a situation just because it's easier?

I didn't see the big move as a father's sacrifice. In fact, another three decades would go by before I even heard the word "love" cross his lips—I would be forty years old then. Tears were in direct violation of his manhood. I saw his silence, not his quiet strength. It would take the loss of my best friend in a fiery crash and becoming a father myself to help me understand my own father.

Dad grew up in a house that was run by my Grandma O, who probably could have been a drill sergeant for the Army. According to my dad, Grandma O made sure the house was spotless and that there was never a blade of grass out of place out in the yard. If you left a mess, you were in a lot of trouble! My dad told me stories of how each time he left his shoes anywhere but his bedroom, Grandma O would throw them out in the yard. I guess this taught my dad to put his shoes away! You didn't mess with the cleanliness of Grandma O's house or you paid the consequences. Even though Grandma O was very tough, she also was very loving. Grandpa O was a self-made man, a five-decade veteran of the New York Life Insurance Company, a hard worker who started out by emptying garbage cans and then worked his way up to senior vice president. He didn't have a high school diploma, but he read the *Funk and Wagnalls* dictionary from front to back multiple times. Grandpa O was a gentleman who had the handsome looks of a Hollywood actor and the vocabulary of a Harvard professor. I loved my Grandma and Grandpa O. One thing they both had in common was their sensitivity toward my dad. He had triple arthrodesis, a fancy name for people born with flat feet. Dad's feet must have been flatter than flat because he spent a lot of time on crutches as a kid, even missing his grade school graduation. His feet were constantly in pain and swollen from staples the doctors put in. The O's were very protective of my dad because of this.

My dad's older brother Ray, and two younger sisters Lynn and Bettie embraced life with gusto. They all had that Italian zest for life—even though they were Irish and German. My Uncle Ray handed out big smooches on the cheek like candy and hugged you until your lungs screamed for air. Both my Aunt Bettie and Aunt Lynn were affectionate and proud of me, like me saying "hello" deserved an Olympic gold medal.

My dad, though, he remained quiet and reserved compared to his siblings. He kept emotion simmering far below the surface. I watched him, as a child, from a distance. And all through the teen years, all the while my mouth ran off and we butted heads on just about everything, I looked up to him. I wanted to be a big man like him, a strong man who kept his heart in check.

What happens when you cover emotion with the dirt of

everyday tasks? Maybe your heart gets buried. When there's that much distance between you and the way you feel, you sort of lose touch with who you really are. I wonder if that happened to my dad as he drove those long, lonely miles to Texas, leaving behind all the people and things he knew and loved.

I never got the chance to fully explain all that to Tammy. I should have. I think she might have understood me better, especially since she came from a racing family too. Her dad was famed drag racer Keith Ferrell. Her parents were hard working folks from Fairborn, Ohio, a town of roughly twenty thousand back in the sixties located near Dayton. The Ferrells were Protestant, but not regular churchgoers like my family. Tammy was the middle child—but the oldest daughter. She took on the responsibility of babying her little sister Teri like it was a mission in life while always encouraging her older brother Tim as he pursued a career in racing. She proved to be a strong writer, class of '77 from Baker High School, where she kept her naturally dark brown hair cut short and feathered like Shirley Jones in the classic *Partridge Family* sitcom. Her dad not only raced cars, he worked for different people who raced, which kept him on the road a lot, away from his family. Tammy came to accept distance in many, many ways throughout her life.

***

Once I was old enough to know the difference between a clutch and an engine, I was at the shop cleaning up and learning how to work on cars. My dad got me up early on Saturday mornings to go down to the shop. We'd get cars ready, go to lunch with friends or even go to somebody else's place. I didn't mind. I would have just been home watching TV or sleeping anyway.

I continued pitching and playing third base, even winning another Little League championship in Texas. But as I grew older, my time became more and more tied up with Dad's shop until I eventually just left my mitt and bat bag in the garage to collect dust. I didn't realize I wasn't living the life of an everyday kid until I became a teenager and noticed that my friends were serving up pizzas at places like the local Pizza Inn and making out with cute girls underneath the bleachers during Friday night football games. I wanted to do all that, too, but my dad had other ideas. Even in the summer I would spend time at the shop cleaning up or sanding cars, getting them ready for paint. Jon O's and my room were covered with hundreds of autographed handout cards—pictures showing the race car or driver or both— thumbtacked to our walls right alongside posters of Lonnie Anderson and Farrah Fawcett. Our life was cluttered with those cards.

While my time at the track shaped my love of racing, I also sensed I was missing something.

Sometimes, I've wondered if people thought I didn't have it in me to be anything else but the shop owner's son. Maybe people—you know, parents of my friends, teachers, neighbors— thought that was all I could ever be. These aren't big deals, but they do cross my mind now and then on nights I can't sleep.

As I look back, I realize my dad wanted the best for me and the best out of me. He wanted me to be involved with the things he was passionate about, maybe he even saw me following in his footsteps with the business someday. This I know for sure:

My mom and dad worked very hard to keep us kids fed and keep clothes on our backs. It was tough for them being so far away from family. But I don't think either of my parents ever regretted leaving Jersey. They simply put family first.

Dad and I never talked about these things. Actually, that list was pretty long. We didn't talk about girls or life after high school or how I wished I could play football or get a crappy job that didn't pay much like other teenagers. And he never opened up about how hard it was to pay the mortgage or if he ever looked back at the Nirvana or Pleasure Seekers cars or how he felt about me as his son.

Legendary North Carolina State University basketball coach Jimmy Valvano, in a speech he gave after being diagnosed with terminal cancer in 1993, said, "If you laugh, you think, you cry, that's a full day. That's a heck of a day." He was right. In fact, when you think about it, if you string up all those days, it makes a heck of a life.

It would be a very long time before I would see Jimmy V's point or appreciate my dad's sacrifice or even understand what a full day really meant.

That's why you and I are kicking back and spending some time together here. I hope my story helps you become the person you want to be and were meant to be and that you learn from my failures so you can live a happier life. Cue up the three parts of this story. LIES gives you a front row seat to the hard driving, winning-is-everything life I lived for nearly two decades, a guy who bought into all the lies society offers up on the art of winning and the business of being happy. LOVE shares what I discovered from my wife's horrible, tragic illness and the unexpected love story that followed. TRUTH covers how that experience transformed me as a man, as a father and as a crew chief.

Thanks for sharing this ride with me. Now, let's keep motoring forward.

# BIG DADDY DRIVING

*The fuel for Top Fuel cars consists of 90 percent nitromethane, which is very explosive, and 10 percent methanol, which helps ignite the nitro. In like form, a fire in our hearts can catapult us forward so fast we miss all the people cheering from the sidelines.*

God love my mother, she tried everything to get me to study and do better in school, but books were no competition for the parade of people I saw coming through my dad's paint and body shop in Texas.

Racing greats from all over stopped by to see my dad. Sometimes they brought him cars to paint, and other times they just stopped to shoot the shit with him. The list was pretty impressive: "Big Daddy" Don Garlits, considered the greatest drag racer of all time. He named all of his cars Swamp Rat. Raymond Beadle, part showman, part racer, who owned and drove the Blue Max Funny Car. Don "The Snake" Prudhomme, probably the best Funny Car driver of all time, winning four world championships in his Army Funny Car. Chris Karameisines, known as the "Golden Greek" (he's in his eighties and still going strong racing Top Fuel dragsters). Ernie Stautner, an assistant coach for the Dallas Cowboys back then and a professional football Hall of Famer who played for the Pittsburgh Steelers in the fifties and sixties, used to stop by all the time and visit with my dad. Ernie was a great guy! One time, Raymond Beadle brought sports legend Reggie Jackson, a right fielder for the New York Yankees, to my dad's shop to meet me. Of course, I wasn't there. I was out delivering cars we had repaired to Hertz Rental Car out at the Dallas Fort Worth Airport.

Yep, from high school onward, I spent more and more time at Dad's shop. I blasted AC/DC's new *Back in Black* album on my big ol' Panasonic boom box I had bought at the local Target store while I'd talk about the races with my friends. They never did understand why I loved drag racing more than any sport at school. That didn't matter to me.

One person who came to Dad's shop influenced me more than anyone, though: Scott Kalitta. His father Connie was a self-made millionaire and drag racing legend. He was one of the true pioneers of drag racing. In time, Scott would take me under his wing and help me see my future. But not at first. The first time I saw him, he just had this look like he was ready to pick a fight—for no reason at all.

My dad introduced Jon O and me to Scott at the Cajun Nationals in Baton Rouge, Louisiana. I was sixteen years old. Then, my dad immediately ordered us to start cleaning parts for Connie's Top Fuel dragster. Of course, both Jon O and I were excited to help do anything on a Top Fuel dragster—especially Connie Kalitta's. We did what we were told and did our best to stay out of the way and not screw anything up. At first, I thought Scott was an arrogant asshole and didn't care for him much. He crossed lines of respect with his dad that I could never get away with growing up. I remember Scott looking at Jon O and I as a couple of punks who didn't know anything about anything. And he was probably right on that, too! But, we loved racing and that was a fact. The power behind the Top Fuel cars was intoxicating. Your head would shake and every part of you rattled like you were going to be swept up in the race right along with the cars. If you were close enough, smoke clouds descended on spectators covering their arms and legs with tiny pen-like dots from the black rubber exploding from the Top Fuel cars' burnout right before they left the starting line. Diehard fans would line up around the pits for a "nitro bath" as drivers fired up their cars, billows of nitromethane baptizing onlookers standing just a few feet away. Eyes watering, breathing hard, they'd feel like they were floating away.

Scott was a favorite among the ladies at the track with his spiky blond hair and that shit-eating grin. He encouraged me to stick with racing, like he believed I had the grit to stay with it. He always took the time to talk to me, a big shot like him from such a famous racing family. Like him or not, I was impressed. In years to come, Scott would become my best friend, as well as one of the most famous drivers in the country. Of course, back then he was just Connie Kalitta's handsome twenty-year-old son, roving around the track with that afraid-of-nothin' attitude.

While Scott showed his rebel colors pretty loudly, Jon O and I were much more covert about getting what we wanted. We loved going to the movies. Many of the ones we saw are still classics today like *The Blues Brothers, Caddyshack, Mad Max, Stripes, Cannonball Run, Raiders of the Lost Ark* and *Rocky III*. One time, my mom was out of town visiting her friend Judy in Houston and my dad was taking care of us kids for the weekend. We bullshitted my dad into thinking that *Porky's* was a kids movie and my dad never checked the rating (it was "R," of course). I've never seen my dad laugh so much! Mom was not amused.

***

When I was eighteen, my dad, along with Jon O and myself, set out to build an Alcohol dragster that I was going to drive. What teenage boy would argue with that? We never ran the car, though, never even painted it, because we ran out of money. And, let's be honest, I'm not the smallest guy in the world. Besides, by now I had graduated from high school. I wasn't the little kid itching to haul ass up the dragstrip. As I got older, I was much more intrigued by the mechanical side of racing than sitting in the driver's seat. My high came from trying to figure out how to make cars go lightning fast. Eventually, Dad sold the car. I was OK with it because it seemed like the three of us were always arguing about something having to do with that car anyway.

These were the Reagan years. Optimism abounded. Especially for a wise-cracking teenager with Irish blue eyes. Yep, certain things were set in motion, like the gears in a clock in perfect alignment. And Scott Kalitta was the force behind the most important moment of all.

As we got to really know each other, I saw the good in Scott and the pure love he had for racing. There was an edge to him that connected us. He walked, and often crossed, the line of being reverent and rebellious toward his father. I understood that—and envied how he got away with expressing himself to his dad. I think he saw that struggle in me, too, although I never raised rebel hell like he did. He did crazy stuff and I was fascinated by his no-holds-barred wild persona. I had had to stay in the lines for so many years that Scott brought the Irish love of fun (it was part of my family tree; I'll never forget Grandma and Grandpa O's fiftieth wedding anniversary party. Holy shit! I was amazed at how much those people could drink) to the surface in me more than once.

Shortly after we became friends, he inspired me to go deeper into racing as a career. I worked in the Top Alcohol division, a category akin to Triple-A baseball. They were the best of racing's minor leagues. I got my feet wet working on cars all around Dallas, including the Drag On Charger owned by Frank Cook and Chuck Landers, Texas legends in the drag racing world for their super fast Alcohol Funny Cars. With their shop right around the corner from my dad's place, it was easy to hang out with the Drag On team after a day at the body shop. Dad didn't say much every time I'd hit the road to places like Houston or Baton Rouge for a race.

He always knew I'd come back.

By now, I had learned a lot about race cars. But working on Jay Meyer's Alcohol dragster awakened in me a deep desire to win. Jay was like a cowboy without a hat—he had that soft-spoken, easygoing personality that was big and confident all at the same time. Picture John Wayne chewing on a piece of tall grass while he sets the outlaws straight. Meticulous, methodical, Meyer was in it to win. I'd never seen such all-out, steely, competitive spirit. A spark flickered inside me. I had tasted the thrill of coming in first by getting behind Jay's team, and I wanted more. Jay respected my work ethic and my willingness to learn, too. He was in the construction business so he recognized an honest day's work because that's how he lived his life. I would drive five hours from Plano down to Freeport, Texas, to work on his car every chance I got. He encouraged me by just allowing me to work on parts of his race car that I had never worked on before. It was a lot of on-the-job training. I didn't get paid, but I got a whole lot of knowledge about racing in a short amount of time. I owe a lot to Jay for giving me a chance.

Not long after I reached the legal drinking age of twenty-one (at least I wasn't breaking the law anymore), I worked on Jay's Alcohol dragster at the Coca-Cola Funny Car Classic at the Texas Motorplex in Ennis, Texas, about thirty miles south of Dallas. (I actually painted that car for Jay.)

As usual, I walked over and said hello to Scott and asked how he was doing. Once we became friends, Scott was always good to me. I trusted him. In fact, I felt like he and his dad were the type of people who I really wanted to work for someday. I had long thought about asking Scott for a job, but I was still nervous. I was scared he would laugh at me, or worse yet, tell me no! At that race, while Scott was standing around his Funny Car between qualifying rounds, I just knew that if I didn't open my mouth and ask, I might never get up the nerve. Finally, I came out with it.

"Scott, I want to work on your Funny Car someday," I told him boldly, my hands stuffed in my pockets to keep them from shaking.

"Your dad will never let you leave the body shop," he said as he rubbed his chin only the way that Scott could.

"Bullshit. Forget that noise. I'm serious. I know there's a lot for me to learn, but I know I can do this and be part of your team." Dammit, this is something I wanted so badly I could taste it.

He looked at me and kind of pursed his lips to one side and squinted his eyes like he was thinking, finally saying, "There are no openings—yet."

"Well, I'm ready when there are," I stated with all the confidence of a father's son ready to become a man.

In March 1988, I joined the Kalitta team, just one month after that conversation.

# SIN CITY

*The fuel pump for an NHRA Top Fuel dragster delivers 105 gallons of fuel per minute, the equivalent to thirteen bathroom showers running at the same time. As the lies we want to believe rain down, the truth can get swiftly washed away.*

Moving to Ypsilanti, a midsize town just west of Detroit, seemed more like an extended vacation. When I first came to work for Connie and Scott, I thought, *I'll do this for a couple of years and then go back to the real world. I'll go back to the paint and body shop I've always known.* Working for the Kalittas, getting a consistent paycheck and moving away from home was my opportunity to prove what I was made of. I was nervous. My aim was to work hard and do a good job. The racing world was small. A part of me felt like Connie and Scott gave me the job because of their relationship with my dad. It killed me to think I would disappoint any of them, especially my dad; I just wanted him to be proud of me and proud of something I did on my own.

My dad put my move in the weekend getaway category. He even bet a bunch of his friends that I wouldn't last three months. Needless to say, he lost a lot of bets!

I kind of felt he resented my leaving, like he thought that I would work for him forever at the body shop. After I put in a couple years at Kalitta, my dad said to me in a pissed off voice, "You will never amount to anything up there." I showed him my W2 from the previous year, and he never said another word about it. I wanted to accomplish things I couldn't do at the shop. He finally accepted I was happy with my life. Looking back, I can see there had to have been some hurt there too, a son choosing to separate himself from his father's world. My mom, on the other hand, was happy that I had found my own way. I think she may have thought I would come home once I got the racing bug out of me, but either way, she was at peace if I was happy and making money. Like the day we left Mrs. Maddaroshian's classroom and she told me to draw something other than a race car, she quietly encouraged me to do my best and follow my ambitions. When I left, she bought my plane ticket for me. All the money I had to my name was in my pocket, which was about five hundred bucks.

Years later, my little brother Jon O confessed: "When we were in high school, we didn't want anything to do with each other. But you were always around. When you went to Kalitta, I missed you so to speak—even if we did argue all the time." He always has to add that extra zinger. Well, I guess he missed me a lot because a couple years later he joined the Kalitta team. (Suzie was "just" my little sister. I loved her, but she and I would get along a whole lot better after we'd all matured.)

From day one, I loved everything about the job: the company, the people, the racing. I missed my family, but somehow I felt like I was still surrounded by people who understood me and who cared about me. Scott and I worked hard on his car and hung out like brothers when we weren't at the shop. At Kalitta, you run as a family around the clock. Randy Green was there too. He was a good friend of mine even before I started working for the Kalitta family. He worked on Scott's car and taught me the fundamentals of organizing equipment and how to work on a race car efficiently. With dark hair and a full moustache, he had Tom Selleck's *Magnum P.I.* look going on. He always had the girls knocking at his door. We used to tease him about flashing "the Green grin" to the ladies to get them to go out with him! Randy was one of many people who taught me the ropes. I admired Connie, Tim Richards and, later, Dick LaHaie, Dale Armstrong and Alan Johnson, all crew chief legends. As I watched them lead and shape their respective teams, I wondered sometimes if I could be like them. My first job at Kalitta wasn't even high enough to have a title. I basically did whatever Scott told me to do, which was a lot of cleaning. I also painted a lot of Funny Car bodies because of all the damage we did to them. That was fun to watch and to fix!

Scott's first ever win in Baytown, Texas, not long after I joined Kalitta, was like a sugar high running through my veins. I LOVED WINNING. I had walked in those shoes once before with Jay Meyer, the first driver I ever worked with who had a strategy, an approach to the car, the track, the weather, the race. Scott's win shocked everybody—those of us on the team and a lot of other people. We joked that "hell froze over in Houston" when we won that race in 1989.

You see, we weren't considered a top team back then. Most people thought racing was just an expensive hobby for Connie and that he didn't care about winning. (This wasn't completely true, but the timing did run parallel with Connie expanding his air cargo company and buying his first Boeing 747. The plane business required a lot of his time and financial support.) We wondered if this win would ever happen again and how the hell did it happen anyway? You just never knew with our team, that's how unpredictable we ran. Not one of us could come up with the big idea to sustain our car's momentum. We needed a good consistent combination that would allow the car to run well every time. We couldn't get it. Plus, Scott was never really doing what his dad told him to do as far as the tune-up went, so sometimes we would end up way out in left field.

The more I worked on the Kalitta cars, though, the more I was sure about what I wanted: to be a crew chief on a Kalitta team. That's how it goes sometimes; we find our way without even knowing how we jumped on the path. I remember a saying that was told to me long ago: God calls each of us for a vocation, a destiny of sorts.

While my life's work was all things racing, my real vocation called to me the day Tammy walked across Kalitta's shop floor.

Her brother, Tim Ferrell, had worked at our shop as a chief mechanic (years later, he would go on to become a crew chief for various teams). Tammy's sister Teri was married to Bubba Sewell, a badass Alcohol dragster driver from the early eighties. Bubba, Texas-born and raised, was one of my racing heroes way before he became my brother-in-law. I liked the way he raced and I had always thought that if I ever got the opportunity to drive an Alcohol dragster, then I wanted to be as good as Bubba. Tammy had handled public relations for the NHRA and was living in Dallas when Connie put her on the Kalitta payroll to manage our press (which was mostly bad at that point since the media never took us seriously). She was seven years my senior.

From the moment Tammy started working at Kalitta, I

knew she was out of my league. She was always well dressed. I wore jeans and T-shirts. Tammy spoke very precisely. I always had a few curse words mixed in with every sentence. She always had a smile on her face. I, on the other hand, always had a look that I was overthinking everything. I was rough around the edges. She clearly wasn't; she presented herself differently than I did, that's for sure. I was just a crew guy.

She soon joined us on the road, writing great stories about our team. Her headlines featuring Kalitta news traveled the wire service. Connie and Scott were serious about changing our image, and there was nobody more passionate about our story than Tammy.

Stunningly beautiful, smart, she had sassy short hair and a polished personality that captivated me. My confidence was there when I was with the guys, the cars, even girls who hung around the track. But not so much with Tammy. I pretty much figured she'd never go for me and that she deserved somebody classy like herself. But there was this attraction that I couldn't shake off. By the end of summer, I started talking to her more. And that's when I began thinking about her no matter what I was doing. You know how that goes? When your thoughts start coming around to someone for no reason at all. I guess that's what happens when you're falling in love.

She said things in a very smart way. Like you'd hear someone say in a speech or in a magazine article. All the while she talked that way, she'd look at you with these beautiful eyes that drew you in. Those eyes made me feel bigger than I was, like I really mattered, like what I thought and said was somehow more profound just because she was in the room. She made me feel like the most important person in the world when she talked to me. She was different than any girl I had ever known. I respected her work ethic and independence, too. Tammy wasn't looking for a free ride, like some girls I had dated before. Everything she had, she earned. She took great pride in that. Since the Ferrells were a racing family like ours, Tammy understood what being on the road meant, the pressure of the pit, and grease under nails.

I loved watching her, a classy lady like that, sitting with all of us boys, hearing the bullshit that came out of our mouths, and not flinching a bit. You could describe what I felt as a crush, but it was more than that. Through Tammy's eyes, I saw what I could be. I saw the life I could have. That's different than a crush. That's falling for someone who is already a part of you with no rhyme or reason. Maybe that's love, right there, straight-up. Scott sensed it almost right away. And Randy Green. When you're with people every day of the week, you just know what's going on in their heads.

And their hearts.

I started getting braver with small talk. We'd talk shop: *Hey, did you see that Funny Car so-and-so came out with?* My favorite thing to do was to make her laugh: *How do you take a bunch of morons and make us all look like we know what we're doing?* She loved it when I asked her that. Thought it was the funniest thing she ever heard. Oh my gosh, how I loved to make her laugh. Of course, the answer to that question was Tammy. She made us all look good.

One night, she and I were hanging out at the Kalitta crew

house where I lived at the time. The TV was on. I can't remember the show because all I cared about was talking with Tammy. We were in the middle of a conversation when I just reached over, put my arm around her waist, pulled her closer to me, and kissed her. Well, I didn't get slapped so I took that as a good sign! What surprised me even more than my boldness was the fact that she kissed me back. I couldn't believe it. I sensed, in that moment, that Tammy was the girl for me. I had never felt like that before, this awakening inside me. We made out like teenagers for what seemed an eternity. There was an innocence and a sweetness to that night that lingered long after I took her home.

Soon after, we went out for dinner, talked and joked around. It was easy being with Tammy. Her open heart and laid-back style filled in my rough edges. I was a typical guy in his early twenties: I didn't know what I wanted in a girlfriend. I knew enough, however—mostly from my failed relationships—that friendship was important in making it all work. Tammy and I were friends and that gave us an edge. She'd light up a smoke, I'd grab a beer, and we'd sit there for hours talking way into the night about the races that particular day, movies we wanted to see, music we liked, or the newest restaurant we wanted to visit. We didn't talk about the future. We didn't have to.

We had run our last race at the NHRA Fall Nationals at the Texas Motorplex. It was the middle of September. The crew was starting to pick up their tools and organize the trailers. I had this pounding in my chest like a ticking time bomb was about to go off. I was falling hard for Tammy; she was beautiful, funny, smart, caring. And she loved drag racing! She and I had talked more at that race than any of the previous ones. In my head, a little voice said, "It's now or never, buddy."

Some of us guys were hanging out at the track, reliving the day's races, discussing the setup of the car and how we could adjust it when I noticed Tammy standing by the trailer. She was so beautiful, and she smiled at me, straight on. That was it. I broke off from the guys and just walked right up to her and asked her to be my girlfriend. Shockingly . . . she said yes. To be honest, I was so happy that I can't even remember what happened after that. I hope I kissed her or held her hand or did something romantic like that, but I probably just stood there, kicked dirt and turned a healthy shade of red. It felt surreal that a girl like Tammy would be my girlfriend. I thought I was dreaming.

By the close of 1990, Scott married Kathy, word was out that Tammy and I were an item, and Scott blessed it, probably because he knew he had no choice.

Tammy and I talked about everything. We were rebels together just by the way we never followed the crowd: We didn't care much about money or fame. Instead, we made our own path. We never worried about what other people did or what they had—or what they said. Some people might not have thought we were right for each other because of the seven-year age difference. We ignored all that. We worked hard every day to do the best job possible for Connie and Scott. Their respect and appreciation were far more important to us than anybody else's.

The following year, Scott came up to me and said, "Are you going to buy her a ring or not?"

"I've got this, Scott."

"I'm serious. I'll take you where I went for Kathy's."

"What is it with you? We spend about seven out of seven days a week together, do I have to shop where you shop, too?" I didn't pick my summers as a kid or my jobs or what I did on weekends. But dammit, I was going to buy the damn ring myself without anyone's help.

I was a broke twenty-five-year-old, but Service Merchandise, a popular catalog and retail store at the time in Ann Arbor, was nice enough to give me a line of credit. I found a round diamond solitaire on a thin gold band (Tammy loved gold jewelry), the best and biggest I could get using the most credit. It was simple and beautiful and classy. Like Tammy.

Then I thought about how I was going to give it to her. She didn't really have a nice coat for winter. So I went to Wilson's Leather at the Briarwood Mall and picked out a black leather coat. Again, I spent the most I could afford. A few days later was Christmas. I love Christmas mornings. Just about everybody everywhere seems to set that one day aside to celebrate their blessings and each other. Tammy and I were alone in my apartment. The big box with the coat in it was wrapped up and sitting under the tree. In the pocket of the coat was the ring. I was nervous. Not because I thought she would say "no." I was pretty confident she'd go along with the proposal. And I wasn't nervous because I thought I was making a mistake. I was nervous because this was one of the biggest moments of my life.

She opened the box and pulled the coat out. She was thrilled. I asked her to try it on. She put the coat on, and then I asked her to put her hand in the pocket. I watched her eyes follow her hand as it disappeared in the leather. She felt the ring, looked up and I got down on one knee and asked her to marry me. I told her I loved her. That I had loved her from the start. That I wanted her to be my wife. Somewhere, in the middle of her tears and her surprise, she said "yes."

Later on, after calling my mom and dad and telling them the news, Scott and Kathy came over and Tammy very proudly showed Kathy the ring while Scott pulled me aside and whispered, "You asshole. You had to get her a bigger diamond than Kathy's?"

"You shouldn't have been so cheap, you tightwad," I shot back. I didn't give a rat's ass, either.

Of course, after a ring comes the wedding. We motored through several months of just enjoying being engaged, and then started planning how we were going to make it official. We would have loved a big reception. But we just couldn't afford it and neither could our parents. Tammy loved Vegas, and I had never been so we decided to go there and get married. Both of our parents knew beforehand, and they were fine with it. We never had a reception or anything like that. Tammy had been married at a younger age which didn't last but a year, so to ask her parents to pay for another wedding would not have been right. And my parents at the time were struggling to make ends meet.

So, just one year after getting engaged, we headed to the Mirage Hotel in Las Vegas. Shaped like an open book with a big fake volcano in front and a shitload of palm trees all over the place, we settled in a room not quite sure what all would take place that weekend.

Las Vegas comes alive at night. We walked down to the strip, passed Harrah's, T-shirt vendors, and endless souvenir shops. Several Elvis impersonators were singing the King's hits with high hair and crazy pantsuits. Voices mixed with music added to the feeling that we had been dropped into some storybook adventure.

I had spotted this one place as we were driving around Vegas checking things out. It was a twenty-four-hour, drive-through wedding service with a little chapel inside for walk-ins. *Do you want to?* She's like, *why not?* I was wearing dress pants and a white dress shirt with a button down sweater. Tammy wore a pair of white slacks with a pretty blouse and a sweater. We looked like dorks! Yep, we got married at the Little White Wedding Chapel where Michael Jordan and Joan Collins (not together, of course) were married. It was five days before Christmas. Surreal. Fake white pillars with angels on them held fake green plants. Fake silk was draped over trellises. I think the only real thing in that place was our love. To be honest, it was all a bit gaudy, but it didn't matter. We were getting hitched!

We walked in the place and there's this lady sitting there who was a dead ringer for Robin Givens, Mike Tyson's former wife. She filled out the paperwork, took our check and walked us over to what looked like a floral emporium. The woman was our witness. Some guy, who we hoped was the real deal, performed the service. We each said "I do" and then kissed and the wedding was over. It was down and dirty and quick. No vows. We just wanted to be married. Neither of us was nervous. We knew it was right. After the ceremony, we headed back to the Mirage and had a great dinner at a Japanese restaurant. Over the span of five nights, I saw a Siegfried and Roy show and fell in love with keno, a favorite game of Tammys, and was astounded each time the casino gave me free drinks while I gambled. I thought that was so nice. I officially became a fan of California Pizza Kitchen, a chain of gourmet pizza places. The restaurant was right inside the Mirage. We enjoyed every part of our trip to Vegas and, because it was my first time there, I was like a dorky tourist with Tammy as my tour guide. Kind of like she'd be my guide in life. They call it the city of sin but, in my case, it was the city of salvation. More than two decades later, Tammy did save me. I know that now. I couldn't have seen it then.

And that was the beginning. Had I, even for the briefest moment, remembered where we came from, I would have been a better person ever after. I would have been happy during all the lost years.

Sounds like a fairy tale ending gone bad, I know. But, if you believe, even an ending can change, even in the eleventh hour. When the cards are clearly stacked against you. Like they were for me.

That's when life seemed as black and dark as night, and I thought I'd never see the light . . . until way off in the distance one small star winked.

# CHASING GHOSTS

*Stone, Woods and Cook named their Funny Car Dark Horse 2.*
*After the Mustang crashed, they built an identical car and named*
*it The Ghost of Dark Horse 2. Unlike cars that are solid to the*
*touch, chasing things that are temporary means pursuit of the*
*impossible.*

When we returned from Vegas, Connie never said much about Tammy and I being married. He was never one to go out and buy a card at the local Hallmark store, that's for sure. Everyone at Kalitta was happy for us, though. Tammy was the only female at Kalitta at the time so there wasn't anybody who would think to throw us a shower or anything like that. I had a lot of people slap me on the back and tell me I was a lucky guy, though, and they were right, every single one of them.

So, with Tammy by my side and a goal to make my job a career, I buckled down and focused on being a more productive member of the Kalitta team. Both Tammy and I were hell bent on making sure us being married wasn't an issue with anyone at Kalitta and that it did not disrupt the flow of the team. I wanted to help make Kalitta Motorsports into what many of us thought it could be—a top-notch team. Tammy and I were both on the road a lot so we didn't have a "home" life like other married couples. And we were both very loyal to Connie. Genuine people love working with the man because what you see is what you get. His passion (and voice) can fill a room. He's big in every way, just like any legend. Connie's one of those guys you want to do good for. Hell, you want to take a frickin' bullet for him, that's just the way he makes you feel. He's wholly passionate about the sport, his shop, his team. Jon O once put it this way: the Kalitta teams are Connie's yachts and Ferraris. They are what make him proud. Watch the movie *Heart Like a Wheel* and you'd think the guy was a complete asshole, but that's not true at all.

Needless to say, it wasn't glamorous working at Kalitta. Most people never knew how deep the river of problems ran if they saw us in the news. The media didn't want to write stories about a losing team or, at best, an inconsistent team. She was a badass when it came to cranking out good news, though! She'd send out the press releases and line up interviews with local newspapers, radio and TV. Plus, these were not media friendly guys to begin with. Her passion and loyalty for Connie and Scott were unconditional, and she went to bat for those two on more than one occasion. One time a reporter wrote a story about the Kalitta Team being the worst team to work for. Tammy wrote that writer back and challenged him point by point. When she was out there, the Kalitta team had the most professional, most creative PR person in the business.

I certainly didn't know how to fix the problems we had. They were bigger than any one of us. What we needed was a leader to turn our team into a competitive, winning team—someone who could help us identify the parts and pieces we needed to make our cars run faster. But I was a young man deeply in love. I had everything: a great job, a gold wedding band on my finger and a dream.

Had we stayed the course and not been put in the national

limelight, I might not have fucked over the next couple decades of my life like I did. Be careful what you wish for. Sometimes, even the best things can distract us from truth.

And that's exactly what happened when we started winning. It all began innocently enough before going horribly off track.

Soon after Tammy and I married, Connie hired world championship driver and crew chief Dick LaHaie. Connie was smart. He knew we had the ability to be a winning team, but needed a leader to make it happen. LaHaie was that guy. Slight in build with sandy brown hair, he'd look at you with steely eyes that never wavered and you knew as he pushed up his gold, wire-rimmed glasses, he was constantly thinking. The mindset of our team immediately changed. Meticulous like my father, mechanically smart like Connie, LaHaie took a bunch of misfits and taught us how to be champions. Everyone was surprised (especially us). Most people didn't think LaHaie would last one race with our team. Connie and Scott had a reputation for being hard to work for. Being a crew guy, I didn't understand what it took to be successful—until LaHaie came on board. Being mechanically smart does not mean we understood the commitment it took to win. LaHaie taught us how important every little job or part and piece was on a Top Fuel car. At first, I shared a lot of what I learned with Tammy. I was starting to see the possibilities for our car. It was exciting.

Within a year, we had finished second in points. It was the first time we got a taste of what it was like to win races and be successful and I liked it. No, I loved it. It made me want more. I set out to work harder and make sure that everything I did was the best it could be. I didn't want to let LaHaie, Connie, Scott or the rest of our team down. By doing this, I unknowingly began pushing Tammy to the side in small, subtle ways.

Going into the next season, all of us at Kalitta were optimistic. And I was even more over the moon because Tammy told me we were having a baby! She had always talked about wanting to be a mother. And I was a typical guy. I was like: Bring it on, let's have a family even though I have no idea what I'm doing. Two months into the pregnancy, though, she began feeling sharp pains followed by spotting.

We knew something was wrong, but we were not prepared the day she had the miscarriage. Losing the baby was devastating, especially for Tammy who had taken on motherhood the moment she discovered she was pregnant. She was so sad. For many days in a row, she cried. Suddenly, there was an emptiness, a grief for a child we would never meet. Our baby. Was it a boy or a girl? We didn't know. All we knew was that something had gone horribly wrong. As she coped with our loss at home, mostly on her own, I continued to travel on the road with the team.

The hurt would stay with her for the rest of her life, tucked away in a very secret and tender place inside her.

*** 

Meanwhile, our team was crossing boundaries we'd never crossed before. With a fresh turnaround on the track, we thought we were outlaws afraid of absolutely nothin'. Media and fans started taking note of us, too. It was that season the idea of pain, black and blue marks, and punches to the gut first came about.

It would come to be known as the Kalitta mosh pit, the

signature celebration of our team. While some in the business would like to see our behavior banned, our fans always cheer us on. Here's how the mosh pit came to be.

Just before the NHRA Spring Nationals in Columbus, Ohio, Nicky Boninfante, my good Italian buddy from Philly—about five feet eight inches tall with dark hair—and myself made a bet about who would make it to the race track first for setup on Wednesday morning before the race. Our wager set the wheels in motion.

Back in those days I drove the semitrailer along with Doug Dragoo. Nicky, Donnie Bender, and my brother drove the van. Since we were just driving from our shop in Ypsilanti down to Columbus, I ended up driving by myself. I asked Nicky what time he would get to the track, and he lit up with bravado, "We will get there before you."

Of course I knew this wasn't possible because Nicky, our clutch specialist, was late to everything. The bet was that if Nicky and the van crew made it to the track before me, then Nicky could punch me in the gut on the starting line after we won a race. Well somehow, some way, the van boys beat me to the track that day by mere moments. Of course, we won that race and Nicky got to punch me right in the gut while everyone busted out laughing. We went on to win three more races in a row after that Columbus win, and each time Nicky slugged me in the gut with the same gusto you'd hit a guy for insulting your wife or mother. After a while, we all just started hitting each other after a win, which really made our celebrations that much more fun if not a little scary.

I was a twenty-eight-year-old married man who probably acted like a kid half my age. We all did, and it was great because guys like to hit. Back then, it was four or five of us idiots slugging it out. (Years later, our mosh pits would involve up to thirty people at a time and NHRA would go crazy trying to control them. The mosh pit punctuates every one of our wins—and not just for the winning team. Everybody from all four of our teams join in. That's how we roll at Kalitta Motorsports—four teams that act as one. Some people want to outlaw the mosh pit due to its "potential for injury," or some corporate speak like that, which makes the ritual even sweeter.)

Tammy thought we were a bunch of clowns. She was right, too.

We took it all the way that season, clinching the Top Fuel Championship while winning five races in nine final-rounds. As we rose to the number one spot, Tammy was right there with me and our team. She played a big part in that championship as well by helping put Scott and the media together, which, before all of this, seemed impossible. She and I both enjoyed every moment from 1994 and enjoyed the banquet at the end of the season and being able to say we were part of a championship winning team when, just five years earlier, Kalitta Motorsports was considered the worst team to work for. Back then I was the only married guy out of us five crew guys. It was tough sometimes because while I may have wanted to go home from the shop early and maybe have a nice dinner with Tammy, I found myself staying later so I could hang out with the rest of the guys and Dick LaHaie. I didn't want to miss out on anything as it related to the car. Tammy never really said much about my late nights and, as always, supported whatever I wanted to do.

Winning tasted good. It was a feeling you didn't ever want to have go away, which just meant you wanted to work harder to feel that way again. Winning is a pretty common lie that is very easy for many of us to buy into. At least I did. The more our team won, the more I thought we could do better. Instead of appreciating what I had, I was always looking for something bigger. It was like chasing a ghost.

Before LaHaie, us clinching a Wally (named after NHRA founder Wally Parks), the most prestigious NHRA trophy, was laughable. Now, there was a parade of brass statues featuring former NHRA Top Gas racer Jack Jones resting his hand on a big ass tire.

As we went into the '95 season, Tammy and I were going to be parents for a second time. She was very cautious about saying anything or getting too outwardly excited about it. As she grew bigger and felt the kicks and slept deeper than she had ever slept before, she also guarded her heart. We took it day by day until we knew that everything was going to be OK with little Ashley O. With the team winning and our momentum growing, the full weight of becoming a father and the responsibilities that went with that title were somewhat lost on me.

Even so, I will never forget the day Ashley was born. It was around six o'clock in the evening on May 14. It was Mother's Day that year and what a present our baby girl was! She was about two weeks late and I was nervous that she would be born while I was away at a race, so we decided to go in and have Tammy induced. Back then, there was an unwritten rule that you didn't miss a race under any circumstances—and that included having a child. When Ashley was born, they found fluid in her lungs. She had to go to the intensive care unit for a day so I didn't get to hold her very long. But when they placed her in my arms, I was amazed that something so small could command such big love. She was a little bundle! With her head resting on my arm, I couldn't stop staring at her. I felt my heart growing bigger by the second. She looked sleepy and that made me smile. She did a big thing coming into the world, no wonder she was tired! Her little fingers wrapped themselves around mine. Her clear, ocean blue eyes drew me in. I didn't want to give her back to the nurse, but I had no choice. After that, I was like a dog chasing its tail because I didn't know what to do as a father. Tammy had read all the baby books, but I didn't even know where they were in our house.

Tammy wanted to name her Olivia, but I was set on Ashley; it was simple yet strong. From the start, she was a very good baby. She was all business, just like her mother. There was none of this crying for no reason stuff. She was perfect.

The relationship between Dad and I changed when Ashley came into the world. My dad was up visiting me and my brother right after Ashley was born. I remember how excited he was to finally see his first granddaughter. He disregarded the nurses who told him he needed to wait before entering the area where Ashley was in ICU; he was like a bull in a China shop!

In the weeks and months after we brought Ashley home, I remember my dad was blown away, and for once, it was for something that had nothing to do with racing. You'd think it was our winning record, but it was more the fact that I changed diapers. I'm not sure he even knew how those white things worked when we were babies; my mom took care of all that. My dad and I started to talk more. I asked for his advice every now and then. I actually sometimes listened without talking back. Things were going pretty good, but Dad still couldn't tell either me or my brother that he loved us. That would come in, of all places, . . . Topeka, Kansas.

Tammy did everything right as a mother. After experiencing life and then loss from miscarriage, she worked very hard to make sure that Ashley did not fall in harms way. It's almost like she had something to prove as a mother—to herself. She and Ashley had a special connection. They could look at each other and just start "talking" even though Ashley's side of the conversation was a completely different language. With me on the road so much, it couldn't have been easy for Tammy to go it alone. Unfortunately, her parents lived north of Atlanta at the time so her mom couldn't just come over and help out. The same went for my parents living in Texas.

***

I didn't fully realize how much I had changed since I first met Tammy until the final eliminations of the NHRA Chief Auto Parts Nationals at the Texas Motorplex. Ashley was five months old, tucked away in her stroller. Tammy had brought her to the track that warm, sunny Texas day. My dad, mom and sister Suzie were there, too.

As I worked on the car, the usual Texas crickets set up shop in the pit, and I focused on my job as cylinder head specialist and ignition specialist. I didn't see anything beyond what we had to do to get that car to win. When I wasn't working on the car, I dreamed about the possibility of us clinching our second Top Fuel championship in a row. The crowds were thick, and most everybody had their bets on us. Drag racing is the humblest of all the motorsports, but we all knew that we had the best car, crew chief, team and driver you could ask for. Two championship wins in a row was rare. But every time I saw the maroon and red American International Airways dragster sitting there among all of our competitors, I felt sure we could do it again.

In the second round, Scott beat one of our closest championship competitors Larry Dixon. Even though Scott's engine was running like crap and on fire, Larry's car was smoking the tires, which gave us an easy win. In an interview right after, Scott grabbed the roll cage and catapulted himself out of the cockpit like a kid who gets out of the pool after ten hours of swimming—only to want more. He jogged over to a reporter, licked his lips and with a huge grin on his face said something that foreshadowed my deep regret later that day, "The win is spectacular. Did we get around it with a little fire?" he shrugged and kicked a cloud of dust up with his feet. "You get over there and it's tough. Hey, you do whatever it takes . . . I shouldn't have done what I did, but we won the championship."

Unfortunately, that line would come back to haunt me.

Our Top Fuel car reached 306 mph in 4.71 seconds against Blaine Johnson in the final-round.

Right after Kalitta's dragster crossed the finish line to win, Scott's parachute slowed the car until it barely came to a stop.

He flew out of the cockpit. Once we finished our mosh pit on the starting line, we sped down to the end of the track and raced toward Scott to start another mosh pit. We met up in a laughing, screaming heap of arms, legs, adrenalin and crazy joy. We lifted Scott up. There were people all over the track congratulating us. The chaos was intoxicating. Scott had picked the competition's pockets with six wins in eight final-rounds. We'd won the championship for the second year in a row and won the race all in the same day.

I had a beautiful wife, a precious baby girl, and I did not see them—literally or figuratively. My focus on the team pushed my family into second place. I'd already upset Tammy early on about something that day. God knows what. I forgot to kiss her and Ashley goodbye? I didn't acknowledge them as they sat on the other side of the hospitality tent? I didn't wave back when Tammy held up our daughter's tiny hand? I had definitely not given them the attention they deserved.

My wife and new daughter should have been my most important accomplishment that day, but I was blind. I never included them in the celebration like I should have, the big win, the two-time championship moment, the team Tammy had helped shape with her smart, well-chosen words. Even though Tammy wasn't at every race anymore, she was still a huge part of us, still making us look good with the media no matter how ugly we could be. She deserved to be part of every bit of that celebration, but my stubbornness and selfishness didn't allow that to happen.

After the win, Tammy called me on that lie, a lie that is

believed in almost every part of our culture, from Wall Street to the everyday workplace. The big lie is that winning is everything, that it's the fastest, easiest and most direct route to happiness.

She marched up to me as Ashley cried in her arms. Whitish, ringed stains from spit-up marked the left shoulder of Tammy's blouse. Tears streaked Ashley's face. "We have waited to see you and congratulate everyone," Tammy shrieked, punctuating each and every word.

"We're taking pictures, Tammy," I said, miffed she could stall the victory celebration.

She sighed. She had a way with words so I knew whatever came next would be spot on. I braced myself, one foot ready to walk away. "To hell with the win, Jim, you are like a bachelor— with a wife and a baby. Start acting like a husband and start acting like you care about us."

By now, Ashley was calming down as Tammy swayed from side to side, holding Ashley close. Our daughter was a talker from day one. She babbled, almost like she had a few words to throw around as well.

"All righty, there you go. Feel better? Why don't you try working on these cars and see if you can do a better job," I returned. Yelling isn't a real big thing with me, but I can ruin a moment faster than a Top Fuel car does a burnout on the starting line. Then, I took one big, fat step too far. I pointed at Ashley, saying, "All you have to do is take care of that little girl. I have all this other stuff to worry about." My last words were the worst: "I'm done." My feet took me one pompous step after another farther and farther away from her.

Addiction can take on many disguises. Most people think of drugs or alcohol or cigarettes. But winning can be addicting, too, like a hit you take to calm your nerves—or feed the craving for more.

I didn't see myself for the ass I was until we were done with pictures; the crowd had thinned, and Scott's earlier words snuck up on me like a thief in the night, tapping me on the shoulder with a big ass grin: "Hey, you do whatever it takes . . . I shouldn't have done what I did, but we won the championship."

Yeah, we won the championship, but I was smoking my tires in the everyday race that starts with feet on the ground and ends in your lover's arms. By the time I realized how badly I had treated Tammy, I felt empty like the win had shrunk to the size of a small, lead ball in the pit of my stomach. Since she flew in with Connie and Scott on Connie's plane, she left as soon as Scott was done with the winner's circle pictures. I did a half-assed apology to Tammy before she left. I owed her a hell of a lot more than that.

Ever find yourself feeling lonely even while surrounded by a million people? Yep, me too. The worst part: addiction is a choice.

\*\*\*

LaHaie tried to tell us, but we wouldn't listen. He said, "The only place to go when you're at the top is down." It is not easy to sustain the highest level, he said. As a crew chief, a husband and a father, I've learned LaHaie's words apply to life, too. When you have it all and don't realize it—when you don't see the blessings and the reasons to be grateful—the only place to go is down. And the longer it takes to feel gratitude, the harder the fall.

Over the years, my dad has told a lot of people how proud he is of me. They probably think it's because I worked my way up to crew chief for a major NHRA drag racing team and a vice president's title for the entire organization. I know the real reason he boasts about me because I know my dad. His priorities were straight: He left Top Fuel racing to move us to Texas. He traded up his dreams so we had a chance at ours. He let me go north, even though he wanted like hell to make me stay.

He was proud of me because I was a father. The title, he knew, required courage. A lot of years would pass before I deserved even a smidgen of his admiration. I needed to be more like my dad, but putting others first was hidden in the gleam of all those shiny Wallys.

# GRAVITY

*An NHRA Top Fuel dragster leaves the starting line with a force nearly five times that of gravity, a force equal to those of the space shuttles that once used to launch at Cape Canaveral. We, too, have an untapped reservoir of power that dwells deep inside our hearts. It's the place where our dreams first take shape.*

Physicist Sir Isaac Newton and LaHaie had one thing in common: they both understood gravity.

After winning back-to-back championships, Scott came within one round of points-leader Blaine Johnson after we won the 1996 NHRA Western Auto Nationals in Topeka, Kansas. All seemed right in our world, and we thought we would get on a roll and clinch the championship just like we did in '94 and '95. After that win in Topeka, though, it seemed like whatever mojo we had found was gone. We went to Denver and lost in the second round. In Sonoma, we blew a tire out in the first-round and crashed the car . . . luckily Scott was not hurt. Seattle, Brainerd, Indianapolis, nothing. We went to Reading, Pennsylvania, and lost the first-round. We got to Topeka and then Dallas, and the same thing happened. Race after race, there was always a reason, an excuse, a loss. We had no idea what the car would do on the track. LaHaie was one of the most consistent tuners in the history of drag racing, and even he couldn't nail down the problem. It would take months before we found the answer. Meanwhile, on both the home and work fronts, blame got spread around like jam on toast. The more time Tammy and I spent apart—me on the road and her caring for Ashley—the more tension we felt when we were together. Our team was no better. With every loss, we began losing faith in each other.

For Tammy and me, there was a constant struggle between the one who did all the work at home and the one who didn't. Tammy was stressed out with all that came with being a new mom, plus working at Kalitta. We had a babysitter on days she went into the office, but I was on the road so much of the time that it was almost like Tammy was a single mom. I could never do enough to help—even though I thought I did at the time. The more this cycle continued, the more defensive I got. Ashley started walking when she was around eleven months old (thankfully, I was there when she took her first steps) so she was motoring all over the place.

Tammy always wanted to make sure she did everything by the book and if something didn't follow what a book said, it threw her for a curve. That was an extra layer of stress and worry that was hard to deal with. I wanted to take those books and burn them sometimes. I would tell her to quit reading them; they were probably written by people who didn't have kids anyway (thank God we didn't have Google back then).

By the time Tammy took Ashley to have her one-year-old picture at Shannon's Photography in Belleville, Michigan, we were getting ready to move into our new house. Tammy decked out Ashley's room in all things panda, Tammy's favorite animal.

We were losing at the track, and, as Tammy's frustration rose at home, there was more and more tension in our marriage. I didn't appreciate what she did or share with her my worries and disappointments. Keeping my heart in check was something I thought a man was supposed to do. Years later, I would find out how wrong I was.

In the middle of all these first-round losses, our toughest opponent Blaine Johnson was in a fiery crash at the U.S. Nationals in Indianapolis during a qualifying run. The Indiana weather showered us with heat and humidity on that last day of August 1996. Blaine's engine exploded after he crossed the finish line, sending him into an opening in the guardrail; his car flew across the track. Not many people know that Scott Kalitta had just made a run and we were towing our car up the return road when Blaine crashed. It all happened right in front of our eyes. Scott jumped out of the van and ran toward Blaine's dragster, and we followed. We were so close that we made it to Blaine before the NHRA Safety Safari. Here was a top-rated driver with a record for the most wins in the Alcohol Dragster Division—twenty-six NHRA national event titles and four national championships—before switching to Top Fuel in 1994.

As I stood there alongside Blaine's car, the screams and running feet and chaos were like hands shaking me awake to something I had never seen before. Scott was yelling at Blaine, trying to get a response out of him, but . . . nothing.

The whole Johnson family arrived at the scene soon afterward and Scott told me to take care of Blaine's brother and crew chief, Alan. Scott told me, "Don't let him near Blaine or the car." Scott knew Blaine wasn't going to make it and he didn't want Alan to see his brother suffer. I tried to console Alan, knowing damn well his brother wouldn't survive. I hoped I told him all the things you're supposed to say to someone who, in all likelihood, just lost his brother. I stood there with Alan as emergency personnel tried to save Blaine. His parents, Everett and Agnes, and his sister Pam, stood along the side in a state of shock, tears running down their faces. I wondered if I was in some horrible nightmare. I wondered, in the far back of my mind, if racing was as big a deal as I thought it was. Connie talked to Dick LaHaie and Scott; he wanted to know every detail about the accident and how we could prevent it from happening in the future.

Then, it was confirmed. Blaine was gone. This was the first major death at an NHRA National event in a very long time.

An ache burned deep inside me. Suddenly, I missed both Tammy and Ashley and wished they were there with me. I just wanted to hold them close and feel them safe in my arms. I called Tammy as soon as I could and let her know what was happening. Knowing how devastated Alan was with losing his brother, his best friend, made me appreciate my brother even more! I hugged Jon O and let him know I loved him and he did the same for me. Blaine's passing was the first time I experienced the death of someone I knew. For just that moment, I wanted a middle ground, a place where all or nothing didn't exist.

With every mile I drove back to Ypsilanti, the desire to be a better husband, a better father, a better brother, a better son, and a better person kicked in. It was your typical "I'm gonna do things better from here on out" resolution that never gets followed through on. When something bad happens, it's easy to think you will be better about certain things. But then time passes. And nothing changes. That's what happened to me.

After our Dallas race that season, it was like the racing fairy waved her magic wand, sprinkling black, sparkly asphalt dust all over our path. The car suddenly started running better. At the last race of the year in Pomona, the NHRA World Finals, we won the $100,000 Big Bud Shootout on Saturday. It was a specialty race. We were in Southern California and it doesn't get much better than that with great weather, great racing at a historic drag racing facility.

We were runner-up at the World Finals on Sunday and worked our way back from fifth to second place for the final point standings of the 1996 season. We had no idea how we got there. What were we doing differently? How did we turn around this hit-or-miss team? In that final race, we made up a lot of lost ground real quick. Then, the season was over.

A few days later, our new clutch guy, John Schultz hesitatingly came over to me. John had taken Nicky's place when he and Doug Dragoo split for a competitor. John was a good guy and a great asset to our team having worked at the biggest clutch vendor in the industry at the time, Applied Friction Technology. I was still the cylinder head and ignition specialist. Taking my job seriously—and with Nicky and Doug gone—I always tried to do what I could to inspire LaHaie's confidence in me and others on our team. We needed to fill in what had walked out the door.

"Can I talk to you for a minute?" John asked.

"Shoot," I said as I stood there in my black Kalitta golf shirt and jeans.

"He told me not to say nothing . . . I was the new guy . . . the problem . . . it got fixed . . .," he stammered. I wanted to bop him upside the head with a wrench just to get him to say one complete sentence that made sense.

"What the hell are you talking about?" I said. I crossed my arms, really listening now.

"Nobody really knew how to work the new clutch grinder you guys bought at the beginning of the year," he answered.

I asked him what he meant by this. "The clutches were off when I came to work here. So, after the Dallas race, I fixed the problem and kept quiet about it—until now," he said pushing his hands deep in his pockets, swallowing hard. He was making more sense, but somehow making even less. How could this happen? Nicky, our lead clutch guy and one of the best in the business, should have been on this. It really underscored the fact that we weren't working together as a team that season. That fact alone made us undeserving of another championship win.

We took the news to LaHaie. He was still pissed about Nicky and Doug leaving, but now it was clear we had had a major problem with the setup of the car and that those who knew stayed silent about it. LaHaie flamed out at us, taking every ounce of his resentment out on the very guys who had stuck by him.

For four years, we had a good, strong team at Kalitta. Lack of communication brought us down. Looking back now, it was the same thing in my personal life: the awkward silence, the disconnect. Tammy devoted her whole self to being a mother. I trusted her to just take care of everything when it came to Ashley. I wasn't as involved with helping Tammy at home as much as she wanted or thought I should be. We stopped working on "us." My work came before Tammy. I wanted to be the best at everything

I did, which included being the best dad. But I took being a husband for granted and never thought about how I could become the best in class for Tammy. With Ashley's personality starting to blossom and Tammy being the parent who was always there, I also was beginning to feel third in line. And I didn't like that position either.

Meanwhile, LaHaie quit and it sucked. I learned something by watching LaHaie. He was focused on the wrong things: resentment toward the people who left and a bad mood toward the rest of us. Maybe this was because he worked so hard teaching us so much, and we just let him down. You can't win championships when you're a house divided by dishonesty. For the same reasons, it's hard to have a happy marriage.

Nicky and I are very close; I've known him for thirty years. Later, I hired him back because I needed someone who knew all of us and how we operated. I knew he had grown as an individual and as a professional. He's very straightforward with me and he knows how I feel about holding back important information. I think he was afraid to admit he didn't have all the answers and, because we communicated like shit as a team, it was easier to just say nothing. Plus there's that little bit of ego in all of us. I learned this from Connie. If we're sitting there and something comes up that he doesn't know, then he'll admit it. But he doesn't just leave it there. He says, "Let's figure it out." If it's OK for a big guy like Connie to say he doesn't know, then it's OK for any of us to admit it too.

LaHaie finally got past a lot of things. He went right back to winning races, and then championships, working for Doug

Herbert and then Don "The Snake" Prudhomme running Larry Dixon's car. Yep, he refocused himself to do what he does best, building great teams.

After LaHaie left the team, my workload, and the pressure to keep our team number one, decreased a little, which allowed me to spend a little more time with Tammy and Ashley. Connie also had quit driving at this point to focus on his business and put Scott in his race car tuned by Ed "The Ace" McCulloch. With two teams under one crew chief, and running just one car, we became very efficient.

So I tried to reset myself as well. As the pressure eased up at the shop, Tammy and I started talking more. When I was home, we would pack up all the baby gear and head to the park with Ashley. We went out to eat at some of our favorite restaurants on nights Tammy needed a break from the kitchen. I tried to refocus on family. I didn't want that third place spot.

Tammy brought the same work ethic and passion she had at Kalitta to motherhood. I loved listening to Tammy read *Goodnight Moon*, Ashley's favorite book about a little rabbit who says goodnight to all his things: a comb, his mittens, a painting above the fireplace with a cow jumping over the moon, even the darkness. Thanks to Tammy's love of books and her time spent reading with Ashley, our little girl was developing quite a vocabulary! Ashley wasn't in school yet, but Tammy talked with her like she was a grown-up all the time. Ashley, in turn, would talk very grown-up to all her Beanie Babies, which she neatly lined up as they took orders from this little girl who loved eating Parmesan cheese, dressing up in her red glittery dress and ruby red slippers, and smiling.

Tammy was always there for Ashley, and she was always there for me. She loved me no matter how good or bad our team performed. She loved me for who I was. I could see she was happy that I was more involved at home, and that made me happy too. Even though I hadn't been the greatest husband to her, she never gave up on me.

The days were getting pretty sweet, and of course I just couldn't leave them that way. Soon, I would have the opportunity to move up the ladder at Kalitta, and it would take a whole lot of hard work to succeed. I didn't want to fail. I wouldn't fail.

Goodnight, happy days.

## WEEKENDS AT THE MOSH PIT

*From a standing start, NHRA Top Fuel dragsters accelerate faster than a jumbo jet, a fighter jet or a Formula One race car. When we get that promotion or A+ on a school paper, ego has an uncanny way of accelerating ever so swiftly.*

The tipping point came at the end of the 1999 season. Ed "The Ace" McCulloch had taken over during the three years after LaHaie left. Ace was a badass! He was known as one of the toughest racers ever because of his many fights over the years. And he never lost a fight, either. He was a five-foot-eleven-inch solid refrigerator. For a guy who'd swing without blinking, he always had perfect hair. He wore glasses and if he ever took them off . . . there was a good chance someone was gonna get punched. In reality, Ace was a great guy with a heart of gold. He reminded me of Connie.

But now Ed was leaving, and we were at a crossroads. Connie cornered me one day. With his hair a little thinner and a little grayer than when I first started at Kalitta, but still leading with that larger than life personality, he got right to the point.

"What do you want?" he asked.

"About what?" I said. It could have gone a couple ways: what do I want for lunch or what do I want from my job? It was the second one.

"Why do you want to be here at Kalitta? Where are you going with all this?" His tone completely serious, his eyes looked into me like I was an ancient relic and he was an archeologist who had spent a lifetime looking for what was now in his hand. I knew whatever came out of my frickin' mouth would change things forever.

"I want to be a crew chief," I said. In my head, I added, *a crew chief like you.*

"OK. I'll teach you," he answered, pressing his pointer finger into my shoulder. "I'll teach you myself."

Done. There were no committees at Kalitta Motorsports. Connie was the beginning and the end. Many people predicted I would fail; they didn't think Connie and I would get along. Many good people have struggled in their relationships with the man who has been rightfully described as strong-minded, strong-willed and a pain in the ass.

But I was confident I knew how to handle him. Like a son to a father, I saw the good in Connie, not his sins, and that was a big difference between me and other people. I loved the guy. I respected him. And I was going to work like hell to prove he had picked the right man for the job. Tammy was very happy for me and very supportive. She knew what this meant to me, that it was not just a promotion but a bold statement about my abilities in the sport of drag racing.

*** 

Gears shifted in the O house. I settled into my new role at work. And Connie asked Tammy to be the office manager at Kalitta Motorsports. He was not the kind of person you said "no" to. Like a tank, he bulldozed forward with his ideas. Tanks always win. Even though Tammy had no clue about accounting principles or many of the processes important to running an office, Connie trusted her and trust was the most important thing that mattered to him as a businessman. She approached the job fiercely, like the perfectionist she was. That was my wife; she was a badass when she put her mind to just about anything.

I never told Tammy how proud I was of her.

Instead, I put my time and thought into being the best crew chief I could be. These weren't our early carefree days, traveling around the country together, blazing a trail for our Top Fuel cars. Tammy and I each had a job to do that was exclusive of the other. A shadow had descended on our marriage, hiding the deep friendship we started out our life with. Honestly, I think many couples who work together experience an extra layer of stress. When you share everything, day and night, it sometimes leaves little room to discover new things about the other person or appreciate one another.

When we did talk, our conversations centered around work. Even before we started talking, we always knew what happened with each other's day because we were there. There was no element of surprise about what we did or who we talked to. We shared the same cast of characters. Sometimes we would get into arguments because of something that happened at work, something we didn't agree on. Like I would get all bent out of shape because she wanted all the damn receipts from my crew guys. Well, she had a job to do—and so did I. Unfortunately, I put my crew chief bravado before Tammy's feelings. I'd say, "What the hell? We've got more important things to do than keep track of receipts. You know what we bought. It's on the car. I'll show you." I acted like a hard-ass over the stupidest things. And, on top of all that, she was right! We should have turned in all the damn receipts.

I'm no marriage counselor, but I'd say too much of the same thing sure made it challenging for us to grow as a couple. Being too close too much of the time created distance between us. We tried to separate our personal and professional lives: We drove to work in separate cars and gave each other space, but I know we should have tried harder. In our efforts to stay out of each other's business at work, we ended up hiding our problems pretty well. Few saw them, and we ignored them. Plus, neither of us wanted to disappoint Connie or Scott by allowing the stress between us to affect our performance at work. Our allegiance to Kalitta Motorsports was of paramount importance to both Tammy and me.

By now, fairy tale stories with happy endings had invaded the O house. Only Ashley was buying it hook, line and sinker as she turned five years old and dreamed about being a Disney princess. Tammy would carefully braid our daughter's hair in long pigtails. Ashley was drop dead cute with her wide smile, round face and bubbly personality. Everybody at Kalitta loved when she came around. Her big blue eyes smiled sunshine the same way Tammy's eyes did when I first met her.

But I wasn't thinking much about my wife and daughter when I got promoted.

My mind was wrapped around points. Elapsed times. Speed. Tuning. The engine. Winning. It was about work, work, work.

Here, right now, my eyes are shut and there's a slow burn

thinking about that time in my life. I'm listening to the rolling, steady drum machine . . . the dry, monotone voice of Phil Collins singing "In the Air Tonight" . . . the narrow sound . . . the in-your-face rhythm filling the far reaches of my mind like an ocean spills into every corner of its basin . . . years later, this would be the song that plants me in the zone before a race. I'm listening to it now. You have to know the whole story. It's not easy for me to think about who I used to be, especially the dark, angry days I spent hurting the people I loved most. But I'm going to try so you can learn from my mistakes. OK, here we go.

When I first became co-crew chief for the MGM Grand Top Fuel dragster for Connie's nephew Doug Kalitta the only thing that made me happy was working on that car and winning. I wanted to prove to Connie and everyone else that I could do this job. Failing was my kryptonite. Pinning my star to results was a repeat of the glory days when we were champions in the mid-nineties. Only this time, we weren't under LaHaie, we were under me and Connie. Almost immediately, I identified with being a co-crew chief more than being a husband to Tammy or a father to Ashley. The longing to win was insatiable and the more I searched to find happiness on the race track, the more elusive the thrill of laughing or feeling loved became. The track became a shrine, like Wally, a false god to worship.

Sure, our family went to Disney and Hawaii and I was bringing home a good paycheck, but I took a lot of what Tammy did as a mother for granted. I never thought about how hard it was to raise a child day in and day out. Tammy didn't have family close by, and she always put on a good front, like life was easy when it really wasn't. She struggled with always having to be the decision maker as a parent, the one on the front lines to figure it all out.

When we lost, I was mad. I blamed myself. Over and over in my mind, I tried to think of what I could do or say to improve our tune-up decisions. I wanted to prove to Connie that I belonged being his right hand man. When there was a loss, I took it personally.

Of course, according to Grandma Hovenac, nothing was my fault. I always visited her and Grandpa Hovenac when we were racing in Jersey. I just wish both of them could have made the trip down to Englishtown to watch us race, but they just couldn't. They did however watch it on TV, and Grandma kept notes for the next time we would talk on the phone. If the car smoked the tires because we had too much clutch on the car, she'd blame it on Doug or Scott. I'd say, "Grandma, it was my fault. They had nothing to do with smoking the tires," and she'd say, "Jimmy, that's not true. They must be doing something wrong so tell them to get it right next time." Oh. My. Gosh. I'd just shake my head and smile. She thought her first grandson was perfect.

For the first four years of the new millennium, we won a lot of races running just Doug's car. Late in 2003 Scott came out of a short-lived retirement and our team grew to two cars. By the time the 2004 season started, we added a third car driven by Dave Grubnic. We now had three top five cars that made a run for the championship each year. All of our teams were running great and the only place I wanted to be was in the winner's circle in cities like Pomona and Englishtown and Dallas. I was looking for running the lowest elapsed time and feeling that high of beating someone else on the track.

When Tammy switched from public relations to office manager for Kalitta, she stopped coming to a lot of the races. That lack of physically being there with us on the road made her feel less a part of the team, like we were slugging it out without her. There were a lot of times when we really enjoyed being with each other, but the difficult or bad times often outweighed the good. We put on a convincing show to the outside world. Privately, though, I'm sure Tammy would talk with her sister Teri about the struggles we had. Of the different issues, one big point of contention was Tammy's smoking. I didn't care for it much when we first met, but after Ashley was born, I asked Tammy more than once to quit. Even though she was down to a few cigarettes a day, I still wasn't happy about it. We took the easiest road for couples who aren't really on the same page, the default route: We avoided talking about things that bothered us because we didn't want to end up arguing.

I was at the shop constantly, working on the cars, working with my crew, analyzing the setup, turning every component of the car over and over in my mind until I'd memorized each shape and placement. I had a point to prove. My life with Tammy and Ashley took a backseat for the second time in my life. The problem is, you don't realize you're fucking up while you're actually fucking up. You get pulled under without seeing the tide. Tunnel vision they call it.

Plus, I had to do well in order to bring home a paycheck. The risk of not doing a good job also meant not having one.

Racing was all I knew.

I felt a nagging desire deep inside me to please Connie just like I'd always tried to please my dad by working in his shop while I was growing up. Connie, a man who had raced longer than I was alive, was a big player in my life. I have learned many things by watching how he handles life. He's an amazing guy. People don't give him the credit he deserves. He and Scott believed in me. Connie barks; people hide, and I never did. My close friend, Cowboy Bob Coffman, one of the craziest and wisest and most trustworthy of all the bad boys (a couple inches shy of an NBA player and at 250 pounds, plus a few extra for the hat, he really looks like a badass too) once described what it was like being with me and Connie: "They ask me to hang out, but then Connie's yelling at Jim O about tune-ups, what has to be done, and who blew up the car and Jim O's yelling right back at him and I'm like 'Thanks, guys, for keeping me here. This is fun.' At the end of the day, they both laugh and say they are sorry."

"Now, Jim O," he always tells me, "that's a family."

I can't argue with Cowboy Bob (I don't think anybody's called him by just his real name since his first pair of boots and spurs at around age four). But I was wrong in treating people at work like all I wanted from them was a win. When we'd lose, I'd sometimes spout off at the crew or just walk away in disappointed silence. In those instances, morale nosedived. It was a shallow way to lead.

At the time, we had a 50,000-square-foot shop, but we were using a little less than half the space. Early on, I said, "Connie, we're going to need this whole building because I'm going to fill it with race cars."

And that's all I saw. The most important thing in the world to me was winning a Top Fuel world championship. I sacrificed time with my wife and my daughter. I not only missed seeing Ashley do so many things for the first time, I missed understanding the thrill of being there to see them take place. It wasn't so much that I was not physically there to see her off on her first day of kindergarten—many fathers travel or work late hours. It was that racing came before big moments like that in my head. And as for Tammy, I missed out on all the little conversations we could have shared about being parents of a beautiful baby girl, where life was taking us, our challenges, the stuff of life's real mosh pit, the place where a person finds real happiness.

Years later, I'd get a wake-up call in a little town on the East Coast. It would be the first time I ever lost someone I truly loved. For now, though, I marched forward. Kind of like a dog that wanders far away from home with no one and nothing to guide him home.

*** 

You can't live in the Kalitta mosh pit twenty-four hours a day. You know why? First of all, it's physically impossible. It hurts. A couple dozen people sprint to an invisible center, each lost in a combative collision of arms, legs, force, pain, exhilaration, chaos and celebration. See why a mosh is so short-lived? (I love it, but it scares the hell out of me all at the same time.)

In our heyday, we won a lot of races and many of us at Kalitta wore black and blue badges of honor because of the mosh pits. The thing is, bruises fade to yellow and then, eventually disappear. The thrill of winning disappears like an ocean wave washes up on the shore, erasing whatever words are written in the sand. Unfortunately, regret is never that temporary.

Phil's song, it's playing in the back of my mind . . . *it's the first time, the last time we ever met.*

First time, last time we ever met . . . why can't today be as sweet as the first time you saw your lover, the first time you said goodbye and felt that rush of pain, the first time you felt truly whole when the other person was in your arms? The kisses from your wife or a hand-drawn picture from your daughter or a backyard barbecue with your buddies, those are the prizes I missed.

Yep, you lose happiness when it's based on things you can't sustain. From every win, every record broken for speed and endurance, every intelligent tuning that could not have gone better, I felt emptier and emptier. A good day hinged on races won. And nobody can win all the time. The real mosh pit of life, a place where happiness comes from having everything you want and everything you need and all that other stuff is just icing on the cake, wasn't in my line of sight. I was focused on society's definition of winning, something that came outside myself, something I couldn't control. It was like pouring oil—outside of the engine.

Tammy walked a lonely road. She kept a lot to herself, and I wasn't there for her. She needed a sounding board, someone to tell her that everything was going to be all right. As Ashley grew older and a little more independent, Tammy, like many moms, felt like she wasn't needed quite as much. Not at home nor at

Kalitta Motorsports nor in our marriage. Isolation, feeling like you're in the fight alone, can be a very hopeless, sad island. She never complained when I stayed an extra day or so after a race to test, when I missed Ashley's dance recitals, when I ate dinner out with the team instead of coming home, when I took work phone calls right before we turned out the light . . . the list, as you can see, is long.

The days, though, for any of us, are super short.

I missed out on having a deeper friendship with Tammy, a bonus category that I think comes after years of marriage between two people who are fully vested.

She loved me, though, so she put her own needs aside. She didn't demand or threaten because she always wanted me to be happy. I guess we both thought racing and winning and stuff like that defined happiness. Later, we would bleed tears realizing how very wrong we were.

Things were changing at Kalitta Motorsports. Our team was growing just the way I had hoped it would. Not only was I vice president of operations for Kalitta Motorsports, I became crew chief for our new driver Hillary Will, mainly because Connie and Scott decided that we needed a Funny Car under the Kalitta banner. Scott would be driving that car. Scott always missed driving Funny Cars and wanted to get back in one for years.

Hillary's car was owned by Ken Black and managed by Kalitta Motorsports. We ran her car from 2006 through 2008. We only won one NHRA race in those three years, but we learned a lot in each race. Hillary had a drive and passion to compete, but not the experience to perform in a Top Fuel car; she just needed reps. Well, we all have to start some place. Many people, from tech people to other drivers told her she would fail, but she went right back at it weekend after weekend, gaining momentum with every race. Tammy loved the fire and drive Hillary had inside her. Thinking back, the two were a lot alike in that way.

# THE SHIP, THE SAIL AND THE WIND

*It takes a Top Fuel dragster 0.8 seconds to reach one hundred mph. In contrast, the heart does not function on time or speed; it is simply very full or very spacious.*

We all know that it's entirely possible to climb in your car, drive to work and get into an accident because some asshole hits you from behind at a stoplight. It's possible, right? Driving has a risk to it. You know about that risk, but the river of life moves you along and you think everything is going to be all right because . . . everything's always been all right.

Until the day you lose someone you love. Then, suddenly, you wake up. You very clearly see the possibility of danger. You never thought it would touch you, but it does. Heartache trades places with innocence. That's how it was for me. I always knew racing was risky business. What I didn't know was my best friend, my big brother Scott Kalitta would give up his life because of those risks. It was June 21, 2008, the final qualifying round for the Lucas Oil NHRA SuperNationals at Old Bridge Township Raceway Park in Englishtown, New Jersey.

You always think the superheroes in your life are untouchable.

I had just gotten back to my trailer after we smoked the tires with Hillary's car. The signal on the radio sputtered so I couldn't hear what was going on at the track. I knew that Scott wasn't qualified yet in his DHL Funny Car, but I felt they would make a good pass and get in the show. As I sat looking at the computer info from Hillary's last run, two people from Kalitta busted into my trailer: Rachel DeLago, a petit girl with shoulder length brown hair and a fiery personality, came in first. Ben Marshall's medium sized frame filled the doorway next. With just a trace of a Texas accent, he told me that Scott had just crashed and it was real bad. I jumped on the first scooter I could find, my heart pounding, and sped down toward the end of the track as fast as that scooter would take me. As I pulled up, I fully expected to see Scott standing there pissed off about what had just happened. Why wouldn't I expect that? He had been through crashes and fires before and always came out of them without even a scratch. He was Superman to me . . . and you can't hurt Superman!

When I finally got to the end of the Englishtown race track . . . I saw nothing but pure destruction everywhere. My God, it looked like a plane crash. There was a smell that hung in the air . . . a smell that I had never experienced before. Where was Scott? I ran all over looking for him, and then I found him on a stretcher. As I ran over to him, an NHRA Official jumped right in front of me and put his arms out stopping me from going any farther. He just looked at me and shook his head, indicating that Scott didn't survive the crash. I couldn't believe what I was seeing. In my mind, I thought: *Impossible. There is no way that Scott is gone!*

Soon afterward, Connie pulled up on his scooter expecting to see, like I had, Scott all pissed off. I ran up to Connie. I dug my hand into his shoulder and told him that Scott didn't survive, that he was gone. Connie dropped slowly on one knee and then the other on a little patch of grass by the end of the track, burying his head into old, calloused hands. Everything around us seemed quiet and still. I was down there with him, my arms around his wide shoulders, holding this grieving father who had just lost his son. And then suddenly, like a random wind catches a sail and moves it in a straight line forward, he rose, wiped his eyes with the back of his sleeve and just took over. There was nothing he could do, and he knew it. He put all of us, as well as the sport of drag racing, on his shoulders. He turned to my brother and me as we walked slowly together, looking at the wreckage from Scott's car and said, "We need to figure out what happened." Connie switched gears so fast that it was mind blowing. He knew he couldn't change what just happened, but he knew he could prevent it from happening again. We promised Connie we would do whatever needed to be done, pushing waves of helplessness and sadness down, down, down into the bottom of our hearts.

I never cried after Scott died. I regret that. It wasn't for lack of grief. Over and over, the realization he would never again walk through the shop hit me like a wild pitch at bat. I wouldn't hear his contagious laugh that got us all going. He'd never see Ashley get married or watch his own children grow up. What was the last thing I said to him? I wish I could remember. I wish I had told him he was a badass who changed my life. I'd say it just like that, too.

I didn't like how it felt to lose someone that I loved, and I didn't want to experience that again. The loss made me want to be closer to Tammy. But I kept all that inside. To the outside world, even to Tammy, I motored through it. I can be emotional on one side, when it's good, especially if I have a Wally in one hand and a drink in the other, but I've struggled on the other side. I wanted to be the strong one, the one who doesn't show their hand when things go wrong.

I learned a lot from watching my devastated boss. I learned it's OK to feel sorrow. Years later, that side of me would come out more with Tammy, although she never saw it as much as I wish she had. There's no rule book stating men are immune to loss and disappointment. If I had a son, I would tell him it's OK to cry. I would tell him it makes you a better person and that it means you're living an honest life.

Growing up Catholic, I got all the sacraments that the Church had to offer. When I got into the racing business, my Grandma Hovenac would get on me, "Are you goin' to church today Jimmy?" I told her that I worked Sunday mornings, same hours as a Catholic priest. That didn't sit well with Grandma.

A lot of Sundays after Scott passed away, I'd walk over to the nondenominational service at the track put on by Racers for Christ. It didn't bring Scott back, but I could still talk to him. I told God my deepest, darkest fears, my big moments, stuff that wasn't very important.

I told Scott I missed him.

Like boys sometimes confess to their big brothers when Mom and Dad are not around.

## TANGO

*If the equipment is paid off, the crew works for free, and nothing blows up, each run down a Top Fuel track costs $2,000 per second. Gratitude, on the other hand, is quite naturally and without exception, free.*

I learned a lot from watching Hillary let go of what other people said about her talents, her driving, her potential. I saw a resilience in her that I wished I had. I was very bummed when we had to park Hillary's dragster due to lack of sponsorship. Meeting after meeting with sponsors and business partners, it was like we were chasing our tails trying to figure out how to survive with limited funding. Businesses across America were folding their cards thanks to the Great Recession. Some financing came from Kalitta Air, an air cargo business Connie owned, but, while it was doing better than we were, it too was hurting. I was beginning to feel like I was failing many of the people I cared about: Ken Black, Grubby, Hillary. We just couldn't put any deals together with sponsors to fund our cars. We looked at everything from a team standpoint—total wins—that was the Kalitta way. The numbers weren't there.

I, along with the rest of the crew from Hillary's car, went on to run Doug Kalitta's car. He posted a single win in 2009, the year Tammy turned fifty, another turning point. She downplayed the birthday, struggling with the fact that she was seven years older than me.

Our wins continued to trickle in like droplets of water from a broken faucet. We just couldn't change the cars' finicky ways.

Failure forced me to reevaluate. And I turned to the one thing that had always been there for me, but that I had long ignored: my family. The little girl in pigtails had grown to be a teenager who blasted rap music and was starting to become influenced by friends. While the "O" trio took vacations and would occasionally see a movie, the family dynamics were changing. We were starting to lead three independent lives.

Meanwhile, race after race, the track served up nothin'.

There was this nagging feeling that called from a very distant place. Like there was something I was supposed to be doing, and I wasn't doing it. Do you ever feel that way? I buried it, but every once in awhile, I would hear it's voice and wonder . . . if we could just change this or that, maybe we could win again ... and then, life would be . . .

That same year, one year after Scott was killed, we were in Englishtown and Alexis DeJoria's Alcohol Funny Car ran off the end of the track. I didn't know her at the time, but later on she told me in a passionate, honest voice, "I feel like Scott saved my life." Scott's accident prompted the NHRA to make major changes to the containment systems at all national event tracks. Races in Top Fuel and Funny Car were shortened from a quarter-mile, 1,320 feet, to 1,000 feet. Top Fuel and Funny Car racing was much safer, and it was because of Connie and Scott. Some people change the world. Some people change it even after they're gone, like Scott: #319 forever, buddy.

All of us—crews, companies, drivers, sponsors, the NHRA—were very involved in trying to make race cars safer. We analyzed Alexis's car. It was another big moment for us. Alexis, with her long brown hair and fierce look of determination each time she climbed into the cockpit, became a friend of the Kalitta team. In fact, years later, she would drive a nitro Funny Car for us and Grubby's car would be back in action, too.

Alexis's testimony that Scott hadn't left us in vain somehow made me happy. I would never recover from losing my best friend, but knowing he saved someone else was a gift. In fact, I have learned that the greatest opportunities grow from gratitude, an abundant quality in life's real mosh pit.

***

I came to find myself walking through the front door of The Dance Pavilion, a dance studio in Ypsilanti's Paint Creek Shopping Mall. Tammy and I would walk past it on our way to our favorite Mexican restaurant, La Fuente. The conversation would go like this. She would say, "Let's go do that." Each time, I'd say, "Hell, no," blasting through the restaurant's doors to order fajitas and guacamole for the night, maybe even a margarita.

But there was that one weekend she was out in Las Vegas with some friends, and I was trying to figure out what to get her for an anniversary present. Again, it was one of those rare moments I was feeling grateful about my life. Ashley and I had just thrown open the glass doors leading into La Fuente when I asked her, "What do you think if I got your mom dance lessons?"

"Yes. Dad, that's perfect!" she said, throwing back her long, dark curls. I knew I was on the right path when I saw Ashley's eyes light up like a full moon slices through a dark room. Seeing that meant a lot to me. We spent the vast majority of time not speaking to each other. This was one of those days we were getting along, and I was thrilled about that. At fourteen, Ashley was, like most teens, the smartest one in the room, which led to a lot of arguments and, worse, caused me to just not deal with her attitude and rebellious behavior. Nothing that my daughter did shocked me. I had skipped school and drank beer in high school. Even under the watchful eye of my dad, I had pushed the envelope and found trouble now and then. No, the things Ashley did weren't shocking, they were annoying because I knew her potential and felt she was wasting it. The more I wanted my sweet, innocent girl back, the more she disappeared. Nine out of ten times, the arguments were my fault. I should have been the mature one, the patient one. Instead, I had a hard time admitting when I made a mistake. Rather than saying *I didn't do that right or I see your point*, I bulldozed my way through conversations. Ashley had that same stubbornness in her. We were like two Top Fuel cars coming at each other from opposite ends of the track.

"Let's do it. Come on. Right now," I said. We turned around, back into the sunlight and marched right over to the dance studio next door. "What have you got for someone who doesn't know how to dance?" I asked the lady behind the desk. Bluntness has never been a problem for me.

She showed me the beginner's package: three private and a couple group lessons. "Sign us up," I told her, thinking *I'm going to do these lessons and then I'm done. I can say I did it and move on with my life.*

Let's just say I wasn't motivated to move. When I worked on race cars, I was pretty fit because I was always doing something. When I became a crew chief and then vice president of operations at Kalitta Motorsports, I sat at a desk trying to figure out how to make cars run faster, keep the business afloat and make Connie happy. I wasn't "watching my figure." I felt like I was always buying bigger clothes. I always had an excuse of why I was gaining weight. I pretty much felt like shit because of my weight. I hated that. Tammy and Ashley hounded me to eat healthier and exercise.

Tammy was thrilled about the lessons. Surprisingly, I loved it so much that I bought twenty more by the third lesson. Of course, my competitive DNA crept in. I couldn't just have a good time. Nope. Even my brother told me, "It's just another fuckin' way for you to compete," and he was right. I, with my dance instructor Trish Stuckey, earned an award for Top Male Student more than once.

One time, we were competing, and I had bought a new dance competition tuxedo shirt so I would look like a pro. When I went to put it on for the first time, I realized it was a onesie that buttoned up in the crotch area like a little baby onesie. "All right," I said, "No frickin' way am I wearing this thing again." But you know what? I still do! Other than that one costume, there wasn't a thing about dancing I didn't like. Plus, the more I danced, the more I lost weight—one hundred pounds in ten months. I felt great, and Tammy was very proud of me. Except, it triggered something: an old insecurity crept into Tammy's mind. She suddenly thought I looked better than I ever did, a successful guy who was on the road a lot. The seven-year difference in our ages jabbed her now and then like a wild thorn.

Our culture, it sure does celebrate youth and beauty. Just another myth, another lie people eat up like chocolate.

Unfortunately, I was beginning to believe it too.

On the road, I acted like a man without a family back home sometimes, like my days were an all-expenses paid, mini-vacation. I'd drink too much with the boys, my personal life a world away from where I stood. For guys, it's easy to separate the stresses of work from the stresses of home. One gives you a paycheck, one doesn't. One you spend a lifetime to prepare for, one throws daily curveballs you have no idea how to handle so that, eventually, you feel like ducking them is better than stopping them. Even though there was a lot of pressure to win and maintain safety on the track, it was more natural for me to be a crew chief. I had a certain amount of control over my success there. I'd spent years prepping myself for the job. It's easier to ignore the responsibilities of being a father and a husband because every day is different and it's hard to figure out the right answers. It's easier, especially when you're not home much, to think that raising kids and having a great marriage and dealing with the daily shit is somebody's else's responsibility. Happiness, then, was defined by my performance on the track, the immediate gratification of winning and scoring points.

These aren't excuses. These are mistakes. That's why I'm writing this book. So you don't make the same ones I did.

*** 

If Tammy was here now, she would tell you that I was the better dancer. But the truth is, she was more natural at it. I had to work harder at it. After a couple of lessons, she was out there doing the salsa with a really good dance lead. I said, "What the hell? You looked awesome out there."

She giggled, "Really? I had no idea what I was doing."

I was like, "Well, you looked like you did. You looked great out there."

When she would do competitions or showcases with her instructor, she just looked more at ease. Me, I'm the football player studying his playbook. I'm like, "Oh, crap I forgot to do this or I missed that step."

In ballroom dancing, they say: If you have a good lead, anybody can do well. I still struggle with leading, but I'm getting better. The textbook explanation:

"The lead is responsible for guiding the couple and initiating transitions to different dance steps and, in improvised dances, for choosing appropriate dance steps to suit the music. The lead conveys his choices and direction to the follow through subtle physical and visual signals, thereby allowing the couple to be smoothly coordinated. These choices are communicated by partner connection."

The greater lesson: I wasn't always a leader for my family or a dependable husband to Tammy. My priorities bounced around like a handful of gumballs smacking a wooden floor over and over again. I didn't take on the world's burdens like Connie did. I didn't always have a life outside that building in Ypsilanti like others on the team did.

Holding my dance partner in frame, my hand in hers, one synchronized movement flowing into the next, made me think about my marriage with Tammy. It showed me what was missing. We had become two islands separated by a sea of miscommunication and ingratitude. We had taken each other for granted for so long that our own stubbornness kept us from trying even if we had wanted to.

The lead in the relationship, which was clearly me, wasn't doing his job.

It takes many days in a row for any one of us to meet the person we were meant to be. I would have to sink so low that even my own reflection was no friend of mine.

# A HOUSE DIVIDED

*Early dragsters raced on flat, smooth surfaces found on lake beds, salt flats,and city streets. How often do we remember where our story really began?*

Every relationship takes work, and, somewhere along the way, I had quit working. Tammy and I just gave up trying to make each other happy. It seemed like no matter what I did . . . I was wrong, and, since I am stubborn, I got on the defensive real quick and would stand my ground. There were times when I could have easily made things better if I would have just given in or admitted I was wrong, but that just wasn't me at the time.

We looked for excuses to argue with each other. When we were at home, we didn't interact a whole lot. I would watch TV and Tammy would usually read a book or watch another show on our other TV. It almost became a game to see who could ignore the other person the most. Tammy wasn't one who went on shopping sprees or overate . . . she would simply drive down to Greektown Casino and play the slot machines. I guess that was her getaway. We did talk about separation a few times, typically at the tail end of arguments, but neither of us was willing to take that step. It did seem like we were living separate lives because we each did what we wanted to do on our own. I would go to a movie by myself or a ballroom dance party, and Tammy would go to the casino. To be honest, it sucked living separate lives.

I'd covered this ground before, that's the really shitty part of it. I was wrapped up in race cars, being a crew chief, hanging out with the boys, traveling around the country chasing the next big win and dancing the hell out of songs. I thought things were better if I just went along and played the part of a husband and father, but it doesn't work that way.

Pretending a life isn't living a life.

Commit this to memory: When you face tough times, stop walking and think backward. Remember where you came from. Every story has a beginning. Had I done this, I would have remembered the race in Dallas where Tammy and I fell into each other's arms standing by that trailer. And how happy I was the day Tammy slipped her hand into a black leather coat and pulled out a ring she would wear the rest of her life. And the confidence and excitement I felt leaving a little Vegas chapel holding hands with my new wife.

Any one of those things would have reset me for the good. Instead, I walked blindly forward, my memories left behind me like broken pieces of glass.

As the New York Giants defeated Ashley O's favorite quarterback Tom Brady from the New England Patriots and our 2012 NHRA Season was getting ready to start, Tammy started getting sick. *We ran out of tissue boxes again?* A simple cold, we thought. Maybe the flu? *Get it checked out; go see the doctor,* I told her. I was annoyed. I WAS ANNOYED. What an asshole.

Yeah, that's who I was back then, believe it or not. Amazing she put up with me. Amazing I walked around blind to her feelings, taking for granted the many minutes that were being used up and thrown away.

## TIPPING SCALES

*Just before a race, Top Fuel drivers do a burnout by spinning their wheels, barely moving forward, creating flames and smoke. Anger oftentimes does the same thing. After all the smoke clears, you find yourself in exactly the same spot.*

You start out as lovers. Stolen kisses, little notes, champagne at midnight, fireside picnics. You fit into the arms of that other person, the dimensions of each body a perfect fit for the other. The thought of anyone else touching the small of your wife's back or brushing their lips against yours is unimaginable.

But love ages. It gets older, more mature, crusty. You start taking the other person for granted. Weeks turn into months and months turn into years and life becomes cluttered. The new mortgage, the next job, the kids' schedules, family functions, pressure to perform, old dreams lost, faucet needs fixing, grass needs mowing, car is in the shop again. Love isn't so simple anymore, is it?

Jesse James, Alexis's husband, is a close friend to all of us at Kalitta. (I know what you're thinking, and you're right. He is the same Jesse James once married to America's sweetheart Sandra Bullock. He's also a badass motorcycle aficionado, tatted up from head to toe with a gift for building motorcycles. His heart is made of gold; he and I hang out nearly every race weekend.) Jesse once observed that I was the leader of all the teams at the track and Tammy was the leader of the office. His point drives home why she and I crossed paths so often: two alpha personalities at home AND in the office.

There was no place to block out anything, to get away from the tension—for either one of us. There was no compartmentalizing. We let our eight-to-five jobs overlap with our most important job, that of being a married couple.

Like a wheel on a bike, a cycle of heartache and joy circles inside all of us. Good times, bad times. For Tammy and me, the pendulum swung too far, too long in one direction. I wished I had recognized it, done something to change it. But I didn't. Instead, doubt overshadowed desire. Anger outpaced patience. Resentment crushed compassion.

We had started out as best friends, the two of us. The Little White Chapel seemed a lifetime away from where we were standing now.

Was the marriage worth it? That's what I kept asking myself. Maybe I wanted a wife who took in the town with me on Saturday nights. Maybe Tammy wanted a husband who would flop on the couch, watch movies and eat popcorn. So, you call out to Change like he's the man of the hour wearing a slick, black suit, a martini in his hand, a shit-eating grin on his face tempting you to follow him.

When small things become toxic, Change looks voluptuous. I wouldn't return a phone call because I knew it would piss her off. She would come at me with her eyes blazing because I didn't close the garage door. I'd get on her about her smoking, a habit I hated early on when Tammy smoked a pack a day. It was crazy, stupid nonsense. What was I thinking? WHAT WAS I THINKING? We argued like it was an Olympic sport. Going into work was as tough as going home sometimes for both of us.

By now, April's rains drenched the earth. And as the water, sounding like fistfuls of cellophane crackling under pressure, washed away winter's dirt, Tammy and I argued and argued— especially about how Ashley was acting. The heated words left us raw and distanced us from the very things that brought us together. I wanted to send Ashley off to a strict military-style school that would straighten her out. Tammy was wildly against sending Ashley anywhere. We also argued about how things should be handled at Kalitta Motorsports, I felt like she was far too picky about receipts and paperwork. In reality she was right, but I was very defensive of my crew guys.

So, I drank with the boys after a good day of racing on the road, leaving Tammy back home with the responsibility of raising a teenager. I couldn't deal with it.

Every relationship takes work, and, somewhere along the way, I had just quit. I was tired of arguing. I was tired of always feeling like I was the one who was wrong. I wanted to put my energies into things that I could succeed at like racing and ballroom dancing. My marriage wasn't on that list.

Easter appeared earlier than usual in 2012, the eighth of April that year, the Resurrection of our Lord, the promise of new life, joy, unconditional love of a Father who sacrificed His Son, the pinnacle of our Catholic faith.

I faced Tammy as we argued, standing my ground like I was the only one whose voice mattered. This was an argument that I knew I couldn't win, and it was because I was wrong! Of all things, we argued about what we each had done the day before.

I had gone to a sushi place by our house with a couple of friends because Tammy had been down at Greektown Casino all day. I had told her to let me know if she wanted to grab dinner when she was done, but I never heard from her. To my surprise, Tammy and Ashley walked into the sushi place about thirty minutes after I had gotten there. Tammy greeted me, looking bruised, thinking I had completely blown her off. Ashley ignored me and just kept on walking. Nothing new there. Now, just one day later, we rehashed yesterday's news.

We'd been avoiding each other all morning, but, eventually, you have to cross paths when you live in the same house and there's only one kitchen. We had no plans for Easter brunch. In the back of my mind, I was hoping the sushi place was open.

"You know, I'm kind of sick of always being on the defense," I said, as I slammed the refrigerator door. Tammy looked stunned. Her eyes blazed, but her voice was in check.

*Why didn't you ask me to go to the sushi place?* she asked in a wistful and hurt voice.

"I did," I said, enunciating each consonant much more than I needed to, completely frustrated. Chocolate, our lab and self-appointed most important family member, was spread out on the floor. Her big eyes looked from one to the other of us. "You never answered my texts," I said defensively. It was weak. I should have called.

"That's because you never texted."

I grabbed at shit just to throw. "You know what? It's not my fault. That casino of yours is a higher priority than I am."

"Really? REALLY? That's what you think? Well, I think

racing and ballroom dancing are more important to you than me. It's like I'm . . . in the way, yeah, just in your way, like an obstacle." There, it was a stalemate: we were both wrong. Or, maybe we were both right. That's the sad part. Maybe we were both telling the truth.

It was a very stupid argument to say the least. Most of them are. And on the one day when people should be celebrating forgiveness and love.

My marriage crumbled like wedding cake smashed with a fist. It was heart wrenching and senseless. We had allowed so much distance to separate us that, in the end, Tammy gave me permission to do the one thing I had agonized over, but didn't have the courage to do—even at that point—without her approval. She loved me so much that she stepped aside for my happiness. A world of hurt surrounded us.

In the heat of our exchange, she stopped talking and just stared at me for a long while. After a big sigh, she whispered, "I think you need to move out."

Her eyes did not match what she said because it wasn't what she wanted. It was what I wanted. And I was too weak to admit it. I had forced her hand. She brought her palm to her forehead and smoothed her short hair to calm herself. Ashley was in her room, ignoring me as usual.

I took two steps back, like I'd been punched in the gut, turned around and walked upstairs to our bedroom. I packed some clothes and left. I was done dealing with the bullshit. Troy Fasching, a former wrestler from Minnesota and assistant crew chief on Doug's car, had an extra bedroom in his condo, just a couple miles away from our house. As Tammy sat out on the back patio, tired-looking from our spat and her constant coughing, she smoked a cigarette to steady her nerves. I took my pride, my ego and my bravado as a man and walked.

But as the days turned into weeks, I wasn't happy. In fact, the more miserable I felt, the more I was sure the world was against me, their collective voices pushing, pushing, pushing me further into a corner.

Alan Johnson: "Jim O, why aren't you running the right pistons?"

Connie: "Get your head out of your ass, Jim O, and focus on making this car not blow up on that next track."

Tammy: "What do you want from me? I'm dealing with a lot right now with Ashley. You're not here; you've never been here."

Ashley's high school principal: "Mr. Oberhofer, we've repeatedly contacted you about Ashley skipping school. Our dean of students and I are evaluating next steps for your daughter."

Ashley: "You don't KNOW what I am going through, Dad, nor do you even care. Why did you even have me?"

Jon O: "Brother, you are heading in the wrong direction. What is wrong with you? What are you doing?"

The arrows flew. Fuck them all. I couldn't write my own ticket as a boy, I will write it as a man.

Like a ship lost in a dark, inky fog, I felt lost and awkward and too blind to even hope for a sliver of light. Anger edged my days like a wide, thick, black border around a picture frame. In that frame was my life, all boxed in.

From my room in Troy's condo, at night, I could finally sit in the darkness, alone. The clamor of voices were now mostly in my head. It was one of the most selfish things I had ever done. I abandoned my family. I left my team without a leader.

Even in the dark, I saw the outline of my dad's face staring at me, judging me, wanting to know why I didn't do better. I shook my head. I got nothin', I thought.

I brought my troubles to a favorite medicine man notorious for luring cowards down a road of escape: Dr. Crown, otherwise known as Crown Royal whiskey. Sometimes I would stumble into my place or hotel room after midnight many nights, the liquor made the face in the mirror that I had come to hate more acceptable. I wasn't good enough, not for Tammy nor Ashley nor anybody at Kalitta. And every time I went out on the town, every time I tested my moral character, every single time I strayed further and further from the Jim O I wanted to be, I felt how unworthy I was.

My emotional choices were not indicative of who I should have been, who I could have been. At work, my team looked to me for reassurance, but I was a leader showing up, doing my job, but not necessarily leading. I couldn't give them confidence and trust if I didn't feel it myself. Even Jon O didn't recognize me. Was I his boss, his brother or neither?

I missed Tammy, but I didn't tell her. I was lonely, but I wouldn't let on.

Funny, I found myself texting her all the time—small talk stuff. She was guarded, and I don't blame her. After all, I was the one who walked. She had her hands full, too. Ashley was a hellion—not doing her homework, hanging out with the wrong crowd and getting into trouble. Tammy never wavered on standing by our daughter. In the office, the mood was somber and, at best, awkward between us.

One decent thing I did was always text Tammy when I got home from a race. It gave me a sense of normalcy, a connection with her I refused to give up.

Thankfully, Cowboy Bob was the one who threw an ice cold bucket of reality at me. He told me straight out, "Listen, you're going to fucking stop this right fucking now. I don't care what you are going through. This is the line path you're going to stay in because you take a step out here and you're destroying a lot of other things. People look up to you and you can't be doing that. You can't turn your back on everything you've worked for. You can't throw your hands in the air and just say, 'I don't give a fuck.' You do; that's why you worked for it—your marriage, your job. Enough is enough. I love ya, but if you keep pissing me off, I'm going to drill your ass to the ground. You will make this right."

Now, guys are funny. We use the f-word like it's the only adjective that really matters. Guys talk straight-up; there are no hurt feelings and, if there are, they last about a whole second. We don't overthink things. In fact, half the time, we don't even think. So, Cowboy Bob's words were actually really heartfelt, and I knew it. He saw the good in me, still, after all I had done. Others did too. If it wasn't for all of them, I'm not sure I would have had the courage to do what I did next. Gradually, I began sifting through what was left of my marriage. Short phone calls with Tammy. A text asking how she was doing. We met for dinner a couple of times and enjoyed ourselves. I really did miss her!

I didn't expect anything from anyone. I just wanted them to know I was there.

I knew Change was not a friend I wanted to keep.

I couldn't take the dark anymore.

So what is the tipping point for any of us? When we find ourselves in the middle of a raging storm, so far from home, how do we make our way back? Do you see? Our path is cut from our choices.

For me, the tipping point was facing the truth. Cowboy Bob swirled a double Crown tonic with a lime, on the rocks. I was a long-standing member of the Crown Royal society too. The smooth, caramel-colored liquid bathed the back of my throat. The peak of pleasure lasted only a minute. Melancholy descended like a shadow. It had been a couple weeks since I last talked with Cowboy Bob. We were finally catching up over dinner.

"Jim O. What is the heart of the matter here?"

"Guilt."

"Why the guilt?" he said. Suddenly, I was back in the confessional at St. Leo's.

"My actions." I said.

He leaned forward and put his drink down. The Crown's sharp, maple scent filled the space between us. "You can't go back and repair anything by just saying you're sorry for your actions," he said in a staccato way, like every single word jabbed me hard in the shoulder blade. "What you can do is repair the problems by improving your actions now going forward. Don't apologize for what you did back there," his thick arm pointed backwards. I bit.

My eyes followed his motion, but, of course, there was nothing there except tables of people who were far less miserable than me. "Just move forward and do the right thing, now," he continued. "Quit fucking around. I'm not the example. I don't want you to live my life. I'm not you. I'm showing you what you are doing doesn't fit who you are." He sat back in his chair, grabbed his Crown and added, "Live your life, but … Not. Like. This."

"I understand," I blurted out. And I did. I knew what I had to do. I knew what I had to stop doing. I needed to forfeit selfishness. I needed to change my priorities. There was something I felt for the first time in a long time: a sense of relief. "I just …" my eyes looked back at where Cowboy Bob had pointed. All the happy people were still there, enjoying life, laughing, their chatter thundering in my head. A lump in my throat made me want to toss back up the shrimp cocktail we had for appetizers. I was still miserable, but a small part of me breathed a very tiny sigh of relief. I wasn't doing the happy dance, but, in some almost undetectable way, I had confronted Change and told him he was an asshole. It was a start.

Later, Cowboy Bob told me he saw compassion in my eyes for the first time in a long while. And, if you're wondering, the answer is no, everything wasn't just fixed with a wave of Cowboy Bob's magic, ten-gallon hat. Life doesn't work that way.

Look for yourself. The scars are written all over my heart.

\*\*\*

It was the weekend before she was diagnosed. We were on the phone. I threw the words at her: "Are you ever going to get that cough checked out? For crying out loud, I'm sick of hearing it get worse and worse." The question sounded more like an accusation; it fell much more harshly than I meant. I regretted the words immediately. Hurting others never erases problems. But, like always, I reached for the nearest stick at hand to clobber the issue. On the heels of me being so insensitive, there was silence. She hung up.

I've tried to picture what she looked like at that moment. Did she cry? Did she throw something? Did she call her mother? How many times do we say things and never see how it affects another person? To this day, I don't know what she did. But on many nights, after a long day at the office, when everything's quiet and I have a drink in my hand, the sting she must have felt from being misunderstood and alone burns me and makes me close my eyes and ask her to forgive me for the thousandth time.

For all the problems we had, the PR girl and the race car junkie were soon going to face a predator bigger than both of them, and I wouldn't be able to do a damn thing about it.

I was coming off of a race in Houston. I texted her as the plane skidded forward and the seat belt sign blinked off: *Just landed back in Detroit. What are you up to?* I hit the send button. Nothing. So, I called.

"Where are you?" I asked.

"I'm at St. Joe's getting this cough checked out. I can't take it anymore, and I just want to feel better," she said. I told her I would get a cab back to the shop and get my truck and come up to the hospital to be with her. Once I made it to St. Joe's, Tammy had just found out that she had pneumonia and the doctors were going to keep her in the hospital for a few days. After getting checked into her room at the hospital, we met with one of the doctors who told us that they wanted to check a spot on one of Tammy's lungs. I asked "What for?" and the doctor said, "We need to make sure it's not cancerous."

Impossible, I thought to myself, that can't happen; there's no way that spot could be cancerous.

"Are you kidding? It's nothing . . . ,"Tammy said as her voice trailed off. I'm not sure if I stopped listening or if she actually stopped talking.

Like most guys, I'm slow.

Tammy again had tests and a lung cleaning later that week. A cleaning, by definition, washes away the bad stuff. Kind of like the April rains in Michigan. Good, finally she was getting this taken care of. The Kalitta team was heading to the Southern Nationals in Atlanta the following weekend. Before I left, I asked her if she wanted me to stay and she looked at me like I had three heads.

"Go to the race," she said. "I'm fine." We were still separated, but communicating better. I was trying. At least I thought I was.

"I'll stay if you want me to, I can fly in with Doug and Connie," I said.

"Jim O, go. All right? Please. I'll be fine. You being here makes it harder on me, and anyway, I'll be released from here and home by the weekend," she said with finality.

Ever want to believe someone so badly that you fool yourself? Somebody holds up their hands and pushes you gently away like a paper sailboat on a little lake and you sail away like there is nothing but the sun and blue sky to carry you along.

It isn't sturdy though. It's made of paper, flimsy. The boat will become saturated and fold inward and sink. Mine soon was about to go that way.

I flew out Thursday morning. I texted her when we landed.

Me: Hear anything?

Her: *No.*

Me: *Let me know when you do.*

Her: *Sure.*

She lied on both counts. She knew.

***

The Monday after the Atlanta race, we stayed to test. "I'll be home Tuesday morning," I told her. Thick-headed. I should have known she would have results by then.

Tuesday came, and I boarded a flight home, fully expecting Tammy to pick me up at the airport. Once I landed, I texted Tammy as I normally did and asked if she could pick me up at the airport. Her reply back read: *I can't pick you up because I have a doctor's appointment with Dr. Patel* (her personal doctor) *and then I have another appointment at St. Joe's.*

I replied: *OK, what's the appointment at St. Joe's for?*

Tammy: *You don't need to worry about that. It's no big deal.*

Me: *What time and where at St. Joe's is this appointment? I'll meet you there!*

Tammy: *You don't need to meet me there, it's OK.*

"Fuck that," I grumbled to myself. It's hard to swear like you mean it when you have a dozen people so close around you that you can smell Old Spice cologne. Is she hiding something? Why two appointments in one day? I need to be there with her no matter what she says.

I called her and asked her if I could be there and then, finally, just told her that I was coming up to St. Joe's and needed to know where to meet her. She gave in, saying, "OK . . . meet me at the Reichert Health Center in the lobby at 1:30."

I pressed the red button on my phone. The call ended, and I stared out the window looking at the Delta gate agent trying to maneuver the jetway up to the door of the plane I was on, thinking how maybe I should have stayed home. A thin, barely visible fracture ran through me. Something shifted, but I couldn't figure out why or what.

I got off the plane. I grabbed my bag and jumped in a cab to the shop and got in my truck and smoked it to St. Joe's Mercy Hospital. The wide, tall doors opened automatically. Since I got there first, I waited in the main entrance for Tammy to show up. It seemed like it took her forever to get there. Tammy, dressed in a blue long-sleeved shirt, a black Kalitta Motorsports jacket and jeans, walked into the lobby. I walked toward her and she turned around. We exchanged an obligatory kiss on the lips and walked around the lower level of the hospital for what seemed like forever, looking for the lung specialist's office. I didn't realize she was killing time, thinking. We didn't say much to each other. We were walking around in circles. I finally asked her, "Where is this doctor's office?"

She just looked at me and said, "I'm not sure."

Finally she stopped in front of a bench, put her hand on my arm, and asked me to sit down. "Let's talk," she said.

She looked at me, took my hand, wrapping both of hers

around it like a soft nest, and said in a heavy voice, "I have cancer. That's why I'm here today. I'm having a test done to see how bad it is."

The fault line inside me cracked. It swallowed me up faster than I could think. My lips moved, but no sound came out. My head throbbed like a skillet had smacked me from behind.

I wanted time to stop.

My eyes hadn't seen Tammy for a long, long time, but they saw her now. She was scared. I saw it in her beautiful, watery eyes. I lowered my head and closed my eyes. "I'm sorry," was all I could think of saying, my head shaking back and forth. There were a thousand words I wished to say. I couldn't think of one. I scooped her into my arms. We were broken. I cried for the first time since I was a little kid. Sobbed like a baby. It was the first time that Tammy had ever seen me cry. Both of us sat there, tangled in a heap of pain, my body trying to protect her against an enemy that had lurked behind a mask of continuous, wheezing coughing fits and sinus pressure.

Tammy didn't buckle, though. Not at that moment, not ever. Finally, she separated herself from me. A cold chill passed through me.

"Let's go," she said. "I need to get this test done so we can see what's next."

I followed a step behind her. She was having a PET Scan to determine the type of cancer she had. This was the frickin' mother of all X-rays. It would give us a three-dimensional picture of how far the cancer had spread and how her body processes were handling the disease.

I paced the halls just to pass the hours, waiting for her, thinking, hoping. I broke down right there in the little lounge area at the hospital; I didn't care. I work on Top Fuel cars and they go in a straight line. This train was not going in a straight line. Faster and faster, it was taking me further and further away from where I wanted to be.

I sent up a prayer with my eyes closed for the first time since sitting in St. Mark's pews, staring at the Texas dust flying in beams of jewel-tone light, a boy reverent and good and ignorant of the world's harsh realities. I prayed Tammy's results were a mistake. I prayed for myself, that I could figure out how to help her. I told God to make this go away, just make it go away. There's no room in our lives for cancer. The pieces of my life imploded like the sprawling parts of the Big Wheels Jon O and I crashed when we were kids. I couldn't pick these pieces up though. There was no way to put them all back together.

After the PET Scan was completed, I told Tammy that I was moving back home for good. I felt in my heart that I needed to be there for her. I needed to help her win the biggest fight of her life. She could win this battle, but she couldn't do it alone. I needed to be there for Ashley. I just needed to be with my family.

Now, you would think the arguments would have stopped. But they didn't (check out fiction novels for that fairy tale garbage). Nope, this is real life. The first thing she said when I told her I was moving back home, in her defiant, badass voice, was, "Don't move back in here just because I have cancer and you feel sorry for me. Do it because you love me."

Oh my God, are you kidding? I'm like, "I do love you." And

I did. Never had I spoken a truth greater than those words. It was there all along. I was miserable without her. Well, it took several more arguments to prove my feelings. I was like a frickin' lawyer, always on the defense. And, you know what? That was wrong of me. I should have showed her I loved her, not just told her.

A couple of weeks later, we met with her oncologist, Dr. Stella, to go over the results of the PET Scan. He was tall and lean with dark hair streaked with shimmery gray. He had an easy smile, like one of those good-looking doctors on TV. He said it outright, though, and it wasn't a script; it was real: Tammy had stage 4 metastatic lung cancer.

Translation? *Most people don't make it six months.* Are there options? *Well, there are treatments.* Could we pull the tumor out? *It would be like closing the barn door after the horses already got out.* What the hell is that supposed to mean? *We can't pull it out; the cancer cells have spread. They were hiding, of sorts, and could pop up anywhere.* Treatment options? *Radiation and chemo.* Sounded worse than the disease with all the side effect crap.

The doctor tried to be optimistic, I give him that much. He said she was in pretty good health to start, and that would help. Help what? Help her walk this earth a little longer. Oh, yeah, that's right, the finish line, the one where no winners cross. Why wasn't it on the X-rays in February when Dr. Patel thought it was a mild case of the flu?

The doctor said that, after looking at that X-ray from February, there was nothing to see . . . no spots of any kind.

Well, I just couldn't understand how there was nothing to see in February, but a mere two and a half months later . . .

Tammy had stage 4 metastatic lung cancer! Now, I will say this straight-up, it's true, I cringed every time Tammy lit up a smoke over the years. I never understood it. I never liked the smell of it. I never wanted Ashley to do it. But I never thought it would do us in. Dr. Stella did tell us that Tammy's cancer may not have been caused from smoking. It could have been hereditary as her grandmother died of a similar form of cancer. Somehow, this gave us, in a strange sense, a little peace of mind that maybe it wasn't our fault, but also planted a seed of worry for Ashley's health. Either way, we were screwed.

Tammy was positive, like always, and strong, like always, and said, "We can beat this."

People didn't see her struggle because she didn't want them to. She dreaded sympathy almost as much as the vicious cancer cells inside her. Her own parents didn't know how bad it was. Sometimes, her optimism made me a believer. And she helped that along by scheduling appointments for chemo or radiation when I was out of town. The less I knew, the better she liked it. When I would ask how an appointment went, she would tell me the doctors thought it was in remission.

I didn't know what she needed. We danced around cancer, but we never walked through it. Stubbornness and impatience and denial dug my heels in deeper. I thought, *hey, if you're not going to let me in, then I can't help you.* She was bound and determined to handle it herself. Men are willing volunteers to be deceived. And we have lousy memories. This means that if it looks like a duck, acts likes a duck and quacks like a duck, it's a duck. Even if it's a completely different animal that just happens to want to be a duck. But Dr. Stella had told us Tammy had stage 4 metastatic lung cancer. I knew it. Tammy was very good at downplaying it though and even, in my mind, making it disappear with her nonchalant attitude and keeping all of us at a distance from her cancer.

She never wanted Ashley to suffer or feel pain because of the cancer. She wanted her daughter to be happy and to feel loved and feel like everything was going to be OK. When Ashley and I first talked about Tammy's cancer, I told Ashley that there was a chance that it could be just her and me down the road and we somehow needed to work together and get along. We also needed to get along for Tammy's sake. Ashley kept a lot of what was going on inside of her, probably from watching two parents who had done the same thing. Some of our conversations centered around how we could help Tammy beat the cancer, mainly encouraging her to eat better. Ashley was stubborn, just like me. We didn't want to waste time worrying. We wanted to spend time doing something about the problem.

The upcoming Fourth of July holiday underscored the tension in our house. We always celebrated it at a giant lakeside fireworks party hosted by our friend Rick Fischer, a sponsor of our Mac Tools dragster and owner of Fischer Honda in Ypsilanti. As was tradition, we rented a limo so nobody had to worry about driving after a few drinks. Ashley, Cowboy Bob and a few others joined in. As Ashley and I walked into the party and after saying our hellos to "Uncle Rickie", Bob Lawson, Kalitta's sales and marketing manager, crossed the yard with short but steady strides to greet us.

"Where's Tammy?" he asked.

"My mom wasn't feeling well. Chemo," said Ashley flatly, with a bruised look and a forced toss of her curly, brown hair. Typical seventeen-year-old. The more she tried to hide her emotions, the clearer they were. With Tammy's illness, she was transforming, though, a sliver of courage coming to the surface of a young girl who loved makeup and boys and going out with her friends, but who also struggled with a mother stricken with cancer. I didn't feel wholly comfortable leaving Tammy behind, but also knew she needed the peace and quiet to rest.

Bob, using his ever present voice of reason, looked at her for a long second, put down his red Solo cup full of beer, adjusted his wire-framed glasses like he always does before he says something important and said, "Ashley, I can tell you this: Every day, I wish I had my dad back to tell him I love him. Don't divide your mom and your dad. Love them both. And just know that every day is a gift." He knew the tension in our house. He got it.

"Thanks," Ashley blinked, caught off guard by someone who could see through her feelings. She folded her arms, antsy to escape Bob's microscope.

"If there is anything I can ever do to help, you let me know," Bob said, squeezing her arm with reassurance.

Ashley walked away, respectfully, but with an I-know-you're-right-but-I-just-don't-want-to-admit-it-right-now bit of attitude.

In looking back, I'm grateful Bob talked to her. Tammy and I lived in a house divided and Ashley was caught in the crossfire. *We'll find our way another time. There's always tomorrow. Marriage, it goes like this sometimes.* Rotten alibis, every last one of them.

Yes, the lies would continue a little bit longer. They would be so thick, I couldn't even pick them out from the truth until one day, the very last day of the year, in fact, those lies that I believed for so many years would be tossed out on their tails. I would stand there like a badass Hulk after his big, green transformation, and finally, finally *live* the truth.

***

By now, Michigan's long, lazy summer days turned into crisp, apple-eating days of fall. While I was on the road hell bent for a win, trying to rack up points and figuring out how to make the engine work harder, Tammy was filling her body with chemicals. She was racing against time. I can only imagine the roads her mind may have traveled. *I won't see my daughter get married, but will I make it to her high school graduation? I must tell her to stay the course in school, to be strong in this world, to not settle. Have I said all the right and most important things? Did I tell her how amazing she is, and that I'll always be part of her life as she will always be part of mine?*

After Thanksgiving, our race season takes a break.

By now, chemo was done and Tammy was only doing radiation. She lost her sassy brownish blond hair. I went out and bought her a bunch of expensive hats because she refused to wear a wig, even though she eventually went and bought one. An edge to her fight eroded when she started to accept the fact that she had no hair. You could tell the cancer was taking its toll on her body: she was having a much harder time moving around. But she always tried to make sure her nails were done. Her face though looked as beautiful as ever. Tammy could always pass for about ten years younger than she was.

I started going to her appointments and what I saw scared me: beeping noises that sounded like ticking time bombs, huge machines that looked like they could swallow people whole, and the soft, hushed voices of the medical staff—all centered around a woman who supported panda bears, loved the glitter of Las Vegas and was Kalitta's biggest racing fan. Finally, after all the arguments, weak excuses, and self-imposed distance, Tammy and I began battling cancer together, and that one fact gave me at least a little comfort. I started going to doctor appointments with her on a regular basis. From this, I quickly understood that things weren't as good as Tammy led me to believe. I realized that the cancer was spreading each and every day; it was consuming her body and it wasn't going away.

"Together" is a simple line to cross. Why did it take cancer's threat to open my eyes? And isn't that how it works for many of us? We get a serious illness or lose someone we love or see a friend in hospice and it's like, holy crap, I need to do something about this. I need to change my life. Run a marathon. Make a donation. Wear a shiny ribbon. Or, like me, cry and pray and shout . . . and fix myself. That's right, I wanted to understand what was happening inside of Tammy: how she felt about the cancer, what it was like walking in her shoes. I knew I needed to open my mind like I had never done before and quit being selfish. The cancer triggered the start of something very good in the middle of something very bad.

I don't want you to wait for bad things to happen before

finding happiness. Do something. Today, right now, as you flip through these pages, love life and the people in it without the burdens of loss or heartache. Express your feelings, call someone on the phone you haven't talked to in a while, or forgive someone who hurt you. Feel gratitude for the small stuff. Live your life to be happy. There are more positives than negatives in a day. And if you haven't found the scales tipping in that direction, get a new scale.

Look, I didn't show up for the only race that really counted. There are no do-overs for me. But, maybe after reading all this, there will be happier times for you in the days ahead.

## A LITTLE GIRL GROWS UP

*"Reaction Time" is defined as "the time it takes a driver to react to the green starting light on the Christmas Tree" according to the NHRA; it is typically measured in thousandths of a second. Just as fast, the reaction time of a person who believes in themselves happens in less than a blink.*

Through it all, Ashley was amazing. There had been so many times when I just wanted to ship her off to a nunnery and let the dear old sisters straighten her out. Now, I suddenly realized that the reasons were fast disappearing. Phrases like, "Hi, Dad, how was you day?" replaced "This house sucks, I'm out of here." Ashley put her rebellious ways in reverse after Tammy was diagnosed. We saw our daughter more because of her online courses. She made good, smart choices. She was open to our advice (shocking). And she was fiercely protective of her mother. All in all, we liked her just as much as we did before she became a teenager.

I've heard that children are sponges—they take in more than they let on as they grow. It's true. Everything that is good about Ashley came from Tammy being her mother. And there are so many beautiful things. I look at Ashley and see her mother's meticulous attention for using the proper words in their proper places. If there's a typo on a menu, she'll find it just like her mother. And then you have me who could misspell "cat" and can't see anything past the words "steak" or "fries."

One of the things I've learned in life is that when

commitment comes from the deepest part of a person's heart, there is little risk of failure. Ashley was born on Mother's Day and it couldn't have been more fitting because Tammy wanted to be a mother more than anything else. She was committed to Ashley before she belted out her first cry. In a lot of ways, Tammy was a single mom with me being on the road so much. She never blamed me for Ashley's temper and challenging behavior during her teen years, but not having a father at home sure didn't help.

Youth is a rocky road for everybody and Ashley was no exception. The fights, the ditching school, the questionable friends, the late nights. Sometimes, she was just downright nasty, and I would wonder where the hell the little girl with brown pigtails who used to draw "I love you, Daddy" pictures went. I'd impatiently go head-to-head with her while Tammy gave her only daughter the greatest gift a person could give: unconditional love.

My little girl, the fierce, smart young lady who I am lucky to see at work almost every day now, single-handedly turned her life around. I needed to learn from her, and I knew it. Her extreme behavior and questionable choices had given way to balance and maturity.

I remember one conversation we had right around that time. "You know, Dad," she said with that same gorgeous smile I remembered my mom having, that same tone of voice that wrapped around you like an unexpected hug, "you're not the bad guy I thought you were."

"And you aren't the bitch I often called you under my breath!" I shot back without hesitating a second. We laughed until our sides hurt. "I'm serious, though. You've turned things around. I'm proud of you. Your mother is proud of you. This is tough, what you're going through, what we're all going through. And you're doing a great job taking care of your mother, doing your schoolwork, all that stuff." I hesitated, right at the end, and said, "I love you." We had crossed an impasse that, just a few months earlier, I thought would have been impossible.

A father isn't just a man who shows up, paycheck in hand. A father, especially to a daughter, shows her what love looks like. It took me eighteen years to pull that out of my back pocket.

## YESTERDAY IS NOT TODAY

*The engine of choice for many Top Fuel cars is an aluminum version of the famous Chrysler 426 Hemi, an abbreviated version of the word "hemisphere" which means halfway around a circle. If we motored through life like a Hemi, we might meet others halfway, moving us forward in powerful and meaningful ways.*

Everything was shifting, like a race car going sideways. Nothing was making sense, but everything was becoming somehow clearer.

At the close of the 2012 season, I was wandering, like my friend Alex Cross, my favorite character in James Patterson's series of books, so often does. The city of Washington, D.C., can be burning down and he's the only guy who can save it on Christmas Eve, leaving his family with barely a goodbye. Yeah, he and I ask the same soul-searching question again and again: "Am I a shitty guy or the kind my daughter will actually want to introduce to her fiancée?"

It may lack literary eloquence, but the question is a real soul-searching one for the average guy. In fact, it led Tammy and me to have the best conversation of all time, a debate that would expose the lies that defined my life for so long. I had once thought that being crew chief was everything. Lie. Society says prestige and money and fame are the end all, be all. Lie. If you work a thousand hours a week, you'll be number one. Lie. Men don't cry. Big lie. I'm a hot shot because of my success. Even bigger lie. Worse than all those, however, was the fib of all fibs: believing

Tammy was right, that her health wasn't so bad. Why? Because I wanted to believe her—it's easier to live your life and do what you want to do when you ignore the truth. Well, I couldn't ignore it any longer. I was done with the lies, all of them.

I wish I had known then what I know now. Regret is tough—I hate to use that word, but I made things more difficult than they should have been. I didn't listen to what was going on with Tammy. It wasn't until the season ended around Thanksgiving time that I began to understand.

She asked me to put myself in her shoes. When I did that, I realized she was fighting for her life—and mine and Ashley's. It was never just about her. It hit me that I was there because I loved her and wanted to be there. To recognize that was a big moment for me. The strength behind my defenses melted like ice in the heat of the sun. Gone. I didn't want to live like that anymore. Tammy was dying. It hit me, all at once, that she was not going to be here next Christmas and that meant this New Year's Eve was her last.

Sometimes, it comes down to one, unforgettable event in the chronological order of your life. We suddenly remember who we really are, and we feel this rush of adrenaline to fight for something important, something big. My fierce competitive nature took over for the right reasons. I would not lose this one.

New Year's Eve 2012 was the beginning of the end, and I knew it.

On the last day of December, Tammy took a drive down to Greektown Casino and played the slots. She came home and pulled into the driveway around seven o'clock thinking I was gone already to a New Year's Eve party. Well, I wasn't. I came home instead. I'd spent the day thinking about Tammy, our beautiful daughter, those early days and our life together now. I thought about the reality of Tammy's cancer and the fact that none of us have a crystal ball. And, when you think about it, who the hell needs one anyway when the people who are most important in your life are right in front of you? The epiphany changed everything for me.

I couldn't wait to see her. My God, she'd been there all along. ALL ALONG.

"What are you doing here?" she asked, setting down her purse on the counter, punctuating the words slowly, her eyes squinting at me as if she wasn't really sure if it was her husband standing in our kitchen or a look-a-like idiot. She stood there, frozen. *She's processing,* I thought. *Great. That's how much of a shock me putting her first is. I got a real quick glance at the schmuck I'd been for so many of these frickin' years. I wanted to kill that guy.*

"I told my friends I wasn't going. I'm staying with you," I said. "I want to spend New Year's Eve with my wife!" *The words tripped over each other a bit as I said them, but I was feeling something rising deep inside me. I was feeling noble. Although not something I was familiar with, I kind of liked it.*

"You should go to your party, Jim O. You've wanted to go to this party, so you should go," she said, her voice was getting higher. *Nope, she's not winning this time, dammit. She'll go from reasoning to rage here in a second. She didn't disappoint.* "Look, I don't want you to regret not going to that party." She seriously was not going to let this go.

I told her that I would regret not spending New Year's Eve with my wife more than missing some party. "That's not where I belong. I belong with you," I said. *I almost wanted to look around and find out what the guy talking looked like.*

She didn't say anything. She was thinking. I chewed on the inside of my lip wondering if we were just going to stand there and stare at each other until midnight or actually do something.

Then, for the first time in a long time, I saw a big smile on Tammy's face. Seeing her beautiful smile made me smile!

That was a good sign. With my hands in clenched fists, my arms rigidly angled like a downhill skier, I faced the woman I had been married to for twenty years, the mother of my daughter, the only person who stuck with me when I fucked up, the girl in the green, sleeveless dress who walked across a cold, concrete floor right into my lonely heart. I said, "I love you more than anything. I'm here for you. Right now. And I will be here until you don't need me anymore. And even then, even then, Tammy, you and me will be together. That's what's going to happen, like it or not. I'm giving you the only thing I have left at this point. The only thing I know: my love. And I'm sorry it has taken all this time and all this crap to tell you that."

The silence was deafening. The struggle was over. Not just whether or not I was going to stay with the people I loved or go out on New Year's Eve. The struggle of who I wanted to be and who I was for all these years had come to an abrupt end. I had given myself permission to feel.

Ashley's eyes were wide. She watched us like a bystander watching a ping-pong ball flying back and forth. Finally, Tammy realized I had planted my flag. And that was that.

I took her hand. She giggled. Ashley said something about getting the party started, and we did. The three of us popped open a couple bottles of Dom Perignon and, of course, I drank the majority of it. Tammy wasn't much of a drinker and I sort of ignored the fact that Ashley was underage, which makes me father of the year for yet another reason. From that moment onward, that one night, there was no past and there was no future. It was just us.

Tammy and I piled into her white Honda CRV and drove to a movie theater. My breath hung in the air, but I didn't even feel the cold. We went to see the movie *Django Unchained*, a story set in the old-time West. Dust clouds and endless sky and the isolation of a one-sheriff town reminded me of my years growing up in Texas. It didn't much matter. To be honest, I wasn't really following the story line. I was with my wife on New Year's Eve and loving every second of it. The popcorn's gravelly salt mixed with sweet butter made me feel like a kid on his birthday. It was almost like a first date.

We sped home afterward and, of course, Tammy was doing all the driving because the Dom was still circulating through me. It was almost midnight.

We made it home with three minutes to spare before the line between last year and this year would be crossed. We sat on the couch and watched the ball drop in New York's Times Square. At midnight, Tammy put out green grapes and we each ate thirteen of them for good luck (followed by spareribs and sauerkraut the next day). These were Tammy's New Year's Eve and Day traditions that were passed down to her by her mother and her Grandma Matoski. She had generously made them our family's traditions. Why hadn't I ever seen it that way before?

Finally, I felt like I was doing something right. I never made the best or right decisions for Tammy. But that New Year's Eve, my commitment felt good and true and enduring.

Usually I go from saying goodnight to snoring deeply in just under three seconds. Tonight was different. I held off sleep to make the night last longer. I laid there, remembering why I fell in love with Tammy, listening to the sound of her breathing, my hand entangled with hers.

We had made our own little celebration that night. We had found something that was lost for a long time. We had invited love in without even knowing he had gone missing.

That one night, things were so good.

# PART TWO:

# LOVE

# VERY TINY ANGELS

*A Top Fuel crew chief studies and interprets track conditions like a scientist with his data. But off the track, sometimes you just have to run with hope and blind faith.*

We were losing the war.

Like a couple of teenagers driving straight into the stars, our hands outstretched, feeling the wind's push; we had pushed harder, cutting our own path in the dark that New Year's Eve.

What I didn't know was that the happiest and saddest days of my entire life were just ahead.

Tammy began having more consistent pain in her neck and back. The cancer was spreading. Every time we thought it was somewhat under control, a new PET scan would reveal that it wasn't. Still, Tammy was optimistic that something would change and the cancer would go into remission. Her strength and determination and optimism carried all of us.

It became harder and harder for Tammy to get a good night's sleep as the pain would keep her awake most of the night. She was on a light dosage of pain medication, but it didn't make a dent. Some mornings, I would wake up and find Tammy in our spare bedroom. I would ask her why she was in there, and she would always say that she didn't want to wake me because I was a light sleeper. As usual, Tammy always was putting me before herself. Even though she was worn out much of the time, Tammy tried to accomplish as much as she could either at work or at home.

Seeing anyone suffer is hard. Seeing a strong person suffer—someone tough and invincible—is heartbreaking. I believed nothin' could touch her. Nothin' could overrun her. Often, Tammy would brace herself against the challenge to breathe fully and deeply. And in each new spot that suddenly hurt, the pain stayed, like a houseguest that won't leave, making it harder to sleep and harder to motor through her day.

It wasn't just the pain that kept her awake. It was fear. I was scared too.

I have to wonder if all the chemo and radiation was worth it. Is it better to park in front of a big building, schlep up sterile hallways to a room where you're hooked up to a bunch of crap, feeling sick and losing your hair by the handful? Why, instead, weren't we on the couch watching a movie or at the track shooting the shit or eating greasy ground beef mixed with cheese at our favorite Mexican place?

Don't get me wrong. Everybody involved in Tammy's treatment was kind. They seemed like good people. Tammy was one of many patients, yet they knew she loved Mountain Dew and always asked how the Kalitta team was doing—like reporters used to ask her about our team years ago. She loved the girls who worked in the radiation department at St. Joe's. At the end of the day, though, you knew why you were there. It was like putting perfume on a pig: No matter how they dressed up those cancer rooms with soft colors and cushy chairs and nice lamps to make them feel like home, it was still a room where chemicals and high levels of radiation violated a person's body, making you feel worse than the worst hangover you ever had. You're not walking into a condo or hotel room. There is no fruity drink at the pool. The big machines had a job to do.

Tammy had finished her last round of chemo just a few short months after being diagnosed, with the possibility of getting on a list for some experimental chemo down the road. For Tammy to make the cut, the cancer needed to be in remission for a few months, and that just wasn't happening. So, for the time being, radiation was fighting the cancer, and it wasn't doing a very good job of it either. Radiation focused on specific cancer spots popping up in Tammy's body, the ones along her spine, in her neck area and in her kidneys. The problem with radiation is that you only get one shot at treating a specific area. We were getting to a point where cancer was coming back in areas that had been treated. Tammy felt constant pain in her spine and neck as those areas weakened more and more.

By now, I didn't wait for a phone call updating me on Tammy's appointments. I didn't wait in the hospital halls on cushy chairs or grab a cup of coffee while she had a treatment. Almost always I was with Tammy, whether it was in an examination room or somewhere else. The only time I wasn't with her was during radiation. When that happened, I talked with the technicians trying to understand the job they were doing.

One time there was a lady who had been fighting breast cancer; her cancer was in remission. She came up to me and told me to be strong for Tammy and to keep the faith. I thanked her. The woman knew what Tammy needed from others. And I would not disappoint.

There wasn't any other place I'd rather be than with Tammy.

On one of the days, we went in and the doctor told us about another experimental chemo he would like to try, but when they tested her, they realized she wasn't strong enough to take it. I thought: *You don't have a CLUE how strong this woman is.* As we left that office visit, I pushed down the frustration of the impossibility of it all. I couldn't talk. Tammy tried to make light of it, but dammit, they said she wasn't strong enough for something that might help her. A year ago, it was just a bad cough. A year ago.

January was a month of closed doors. Late in the month, Tammy and I decided that we needed to put down our beloved chocolate Labrador, named of all things "Chocolate." The poor dog was throwing up blood. According to the veterinarian, Chocolate had some sort of cancer and putting her down was the best thing to do.

Chocolate was part of our family for almost eleven years and Tammy just loved and spoiled that dog, and Chocolate loved her. Many times, Tammy said that Chocolate was always happy to see her no matter what, and I know Tammy felt the same way about Chocolate (my track record on this was not nearly as good as Chocolate's and the comparison between me and the dog was pointed out to me more than once). Tammy and Chocolate were definitely best friends. It is hard to say goodbye to someone who loves you without judging you, without condition.

And the goodbyes didn't stop there.

On January 30, Jon O and I piled into the front of my Toyota Tundra truck. Ashley sat in the backseat, surrounded by our bags and her backpack filled with books and a laptop.

She'd become an exemplary high school senior with the online coursework keeping her focused and, thankfully, home with Tammy much more than she otherwise would have been. We made the six-hundred-mile trip from Michigan to New Jersey. Of course, January in Jersey is never the best time to expect sunny weather, but on the day of Grandma Hovenac's funeral, it rained like crazy. While we were in the church listening to the priest finish up with Grandma's Mass, the tap, tap, tap of constantly pelting rain hitting the roof suddenly stopped and a ray of sunshine broke through the stained glass windows in a beam of colored light. I felt like my grandma was on her way up to heaven right where she belonged. I closed my eyes and took a deep breath. *Yes, Grandma, I'm here. I know, I know, you're happy I walked into a church. Yes, I should be doing this more . . . I love you.* My hand instinctively felt the very tiny gold angel pins in my pocket. I usually keep them in my backpack so when I'm on the road they are always with me. But I had taken them out that day and carried them with me to the service because Grandma Hovenac had given them to me. Very tiny gold angel pins. Now she had her wings, too.

The next morning we headed back to Michigan knowing that as soon as we got to the house, the veterinarian was coming over to put Chocolate to sleep. One day I said goodbye to my last grandparent and the next day I said goodbye to Chocolate.

Suddenly, they were both just gone.

January was a long month and it sucked. We were kickin' the tires of our broken down world going nowhere, going backward, actually. Without the sound of Chocolate's paws bouncing off the kitchen floor in a mad dance every time she saw the leash, the place got kind of quiet. Grief settled in, filling up the empty space. I missed Grandma, too, but I had this feeling she was still going to figure out a way to kick my ass in gear all the way from heaven.

Life was going to get better, though. We just didn't know it at the time. Because as the disease ravaged everything we knew all our lives, we rediscovered something that no one could ever take away from us: love.

# STARING AT THE BOTTOM OF AN EMPTY PLASTIC CUP

*Elapsed time begins when a Top Fuel car leaves the starting line and ends when the car crosses the finish line. In life, though, there are only a few markers. Mostly, we strive to make the minutes honest and happy in order to pocket the big win.*

With so much loss, there was so much gain.

I was surprised. I mean, you'd think it was all bad and it was, except ... there were these moments. Tammy and I breathed in late night talks like oxygen and laughed our asses off at other times. Hell, we were in love. Again! And when you're in love, anything is possible, even happiness on a really lousy day. Even life in the face of death.

We were playing a second chance for our marriage. I was walking in those shoes again when I was younger and it was just Tammy and me kicking back and living large. We fell in love because we knew a day without the other person was a day we would regret. I was a lucky guy because I was giving my heart away without expecting anything. Except more days. I did want those. But I was going to take what God gave us because, through the pain, there were these really good times. The pain sucked of course. Tammy was now on a heavier dose of medication because the pain in her neck and back was getting worse.

The sleepless nights, the fear, the sadness, the anxiety ... yeah, of course, these were things we hated and wished weren't there.

Joy showed up, though, too.

I saw Tammy through the eyes of the man she had fallen in love with years ago. Layers had been peeled back like the skin of a bright yellow banana. Suddenly, Tammy and I were invincible. Funny thing to think about when a person is dying, but love cheats death. Love is bigger. It's a beginning, never an ending. I got to know love during that cold Michigan winter.

We all go through these bad times and we think, "we'll get over it and move on. We have a thousand chances to do it over." Then, something happens and you're like, "shit, this problem isn't going away." When I realized that, it made me cherish her and cherish the people and things around me. I had everything: my life with Tammy, time with my beautiful and brave daughter, the chance to race, the people at Kalitta whom I trusted to watch my back, my brother who cared about me (even if he did fight me tooth and nail on the small stuff.), my parents who sacrificed to create a better life for me when I was young.

Another day. Another chance to say, "I love you." Another chance to be happy.

Love. We say that word a lot, don't we? Love. I've said it a million times. We say "I love fast cars" or "I love the Pittsburgh Steelers" (OK, so this is my team; Tammy loved the Cincinnati Bengals—we were an equal opportunity football family) or "I love this pizza" and we mean it, but I'm not sure if love gets watered down that way. Maybe love is so infinite, it can't be described in words. Maybe it's a touch or a look or something so enduring, we can't put it in a box and slap a label on it. Maybe it's heaven and we're all here, living the good life without even knowing it. And it's all the other shit that gets in the way of love that turns heaven into hell right under our feet.

Tammy understood love. She gave it unconditionally. For her, it was constant, abundant, unwavering. Love was Tammy's modus operandi. It always was. I remember a young man, Mike Rushlow, and his father Don who would come to as many races as they could afford. Wheelchair bound, Mike was a huge fan of the Kalitta team and would always stop by our pit area to say hello. Tammy was the first person he'd want to see. She would sit and talk with him patiently. Mike would communicate with a board using symbols and letters and sometimes figuring out what he was saying was like a puzzle. As he pointed to characters on his board, Tammy would talk to him as though it were the most natural way to shoot the shit, like their conversations were the kind she had with everybody. That's love. That's what Tammy was all about.

And she brought that love to our home in big, life-changing ways. In Ashley's most rebellious moments, Tammy's love wrapped itself around our daughter and helped her stay the course. When I did stupid things or was away more than I should have been, Tammy's love paved the road back home. I took a page from her book on New Year's Eve, the best night of my life.

And from that one night, so many other things grew: gratitude, clarity, perspective and the significance of the smallest, most insignificant moments.

\*\*\*

"Hey, Pops, how's mom?" Ashley said. She wore her white, short-sleeved starched shirt with the Steak and Shake signature black bow tie and apron. I shimmied into the booth, shoved my black winter coat into the corner, sighed and propped up my chin on the palm of my hand, taking in my daughter who was standing there, pen poised.

It had been less than a week since Grandma Hovenac's funeral. I had taken Tammy to St. Joe's Hospital for another round of radiation on her spine earlier that day to see if radiation could win a battle with the cancer cells.

"Well, the radiologist asked me how our team did in pre-season testing down in Florida, but instead of me answering the question, your mother chimed in and said, 'Great if the crew chief would get his head around the clutch problem.'"

"Well, she calls it as she sees it," my daughter said, swift, smart and sarcastic like her mother.

I ordered the usual—grilled chicken salad with an iced tea. Now, not many people go to Steak and Shake and order a salad, but since I was still trying to keep off the weight I'd lost a few years before, a salad sounded good to me and my waistline. I'd come a long way since my bacon cheeseburger-fries-and-chocolate-shake days!

"How's school, sweetie?" I asked. Ashley's co-workers knew Tammy was sick so they always gave Ashley space to talk to me.

"I had this dream last night," Ashley said, brushing aside my question. She sat in the seat opposite me, her thick hair thrown up in a bun. I loved our talks. I felt like we were co-conspirators in a scheme to make everything OK again. She continued, "It had a train station in it."

I stared at her blankly. Guys don't interpret dreams.

"You only get so much time," she marched forward patiently. I wasn't good at looking past the obvious. She got that. "What if I missed getting off that train for Mom, the one in my dream? If I had known about Mom sooner, I would have changed my priorities and attitude. I would have stopped hanging out with my friends so much." She looked down, "Maybe I wouldn't have made the choices I made." I stared at her blankly. *What did a train have to do with Tammy?*

She exhaled hard, a clear sign I needed to catch up. "Dad," she said sharply, "you shouldn't have to live with regret. I mean we assume we always have tomorrow and then we run out of tomorrows and then we regret. I think that's why it was a train station; the train is leaving and . . . ," my beautiful daughter was struggling to make sense of her mother's cancer and come to grips with regret. I got it. Her eyes bore into me. That black leather booth with the gray linoleum table between us became our whole world for that moment. I felt humbled she let me in.

"Sweetie, listen to me," my hands open, like I was giving the speech of my life to a crowd of a thousand, "happiness is tied to how we live our life. For me, it's not just about work anymore. It's about everything I do and everyone I love. But . . . ," I hesitated, "it wasn't always that way and you know that. We can't change the past. We can change the now. We can. That's it," I said, feeling more like a real father than ever before. A steady hum of conversation in the place mixed with clanking dishes stacked by a nearby server cushioned our father-daughter talk.

"Listen, you are doing great! You are making good choices by paying attention to your classes, doing your schoolwork, watching over your mom like a hawk, doing your job here. You have nothing to regret."

"Everything has led you to become who you are right now, sweetie," I added. The comment was a casual statement, something that just popped into my head, but it stayed with me the rest of the day into the night and days after. Maybe everything I had done led me to be the person I was too. Maybe I didn't screw it *all* up. Maybe I could leave my regrets behind too. Tammy was holding a flashlight, showing me the way. She always did, all these years. My eyes were just closed.

Later, after I'd finished my salad, I stared at the bottom of my plastic cup. It was empty. My heart, though, it was full.

*** 

It was Valentine's weekend, and all of us met up for the 53rd NHRA Winternationals in Pomona, California. Hillary Will was getting married that same weekend. Tammy wanted to go to the wedding something fierce. She loved Hillary. She made it her top goal to go to that race.

I was concerned it would be too much for Tammy, but I also relished in the fact that she wanted to go. In my mind, I really wondered if the radiation was making any headway. As a crew chief, I was competitive, I didn't like losing, but this battle with cancer was complete bullshit. You go in and hand yourself over to self-imposed sunburn and where does it get you? How is it moving the gauge? I couldn't make any adjustments and see results like I could with my cars. If there was any redeeming part in all this, I was learning the art of patience, a kind of power steering system behind faith. The cancer was writing my script. I was grudgingly learning to give up a little control and deal with it.

I picked up my girls at LAX Airport and we had dinner at a little hole-in-the-wall Mediterranean place near the airport. Somewhat dark and empty, the whole restaurant was ours and we loved it. Tammy and Ashley came out to the track the next day on Friday. Tammy hung out in our hospitality area, waiting all day just to see Doug run. I could tell she was in pain most of the time and asked her if she wanted me to take her back to the hotel. Of course, going back to the hotel was not an option for Tammy's stubborn denial that anything was out of the ordinary. She visited with people whom she hadn't seen in a long, long time, and nothing was going to stop her from doing that! Every time I glanced her way, she had a huge smile on her face and she was always earnestly talking to one person or another like it was the most important conversation in the world, not just another casual exchange of "hey, how you doin'?"

The next day, Tammy had lunch with her old roommate and good friend Rondi. I can only imagine the giggles those two must have had rehashing past adventures. Back at the Kalitta hospitality suite, it was a nonstop parade of people stopping by to talk with Tammy, who was always very positive in telling everyone about her situation. Later that evening, we headed for the big wedding for Hillary and her husband Matt Hines. After traveling on some winding roads, we found the Pomona Valley Mining Company, a cool old restaurant with windows overlooking the sprawling and generous Pomona Canyon. In the late eighteen hundreds, prospectors canvassed those hills for gold. The building looked like two long, narrow boxes with a chalky blackboard finish, one standing up and one on its side. I didn't like the gravel under our shoes; I didn't want Tammy to slip so I supported her arm as we approached the door, hidden a little by an overhang. She was getting short of breath. I could see her struggle.

Biting my lip, thinking as I talked, "Let's find a seat and sit down for the wedding."

After the ceremony, we made our way to where the reception was, and found a couple seats at an open table. "Jim O?" she asked quietly, her eyes greedily searching mine. I held her hand, the buzz around us faded into the distance.

We made it to the wedding, an almost unbelievable feat given Tammy's condition.

"I'm going to get better soon," she said.

"I know you are. We're going to book your flight for Las Vegas in April. You can clean up on keno." I never, ever wanted her to feel like there wouldn't be another race for her.

She smiled. With the festive atmosphere and Tammy by my side, I didn't really know if we were serious or just kidding ourselves. "I'm excited," she returned. "You know what? We've got this. When I get better, I'm going to, A, color my hair, B, get back to work and clean off the mess on my desk and, C, take Ashley out for some new clothes. We haven't been shopping in a while."

Silence.

"I love you," she said softly.

"I love you too," I returned, breathing the words out, choking on them under a tidal wave of feeling, crashing, crashing, crashing.

I let out a big breath. "We have more of everything in front of us. But—right now—what can I do to make you feel better? It's all right if you want me to take you back to the hotel. Whatever you want, honest." I was trying to think of what was best for her physically and emotionally. And, as you have probably figured out, doing two big things at one time is not easy for a guy like me.

"No . . . I wanted to see Hillary get married, and I did, and now I want to have a good time at the reception," she said without hesitating.

Later, Rachel DeLago, our Kalitta Motorsports team manager, and our good friend Rick Fischer caught up with us at the reception after the bride and bridegroom sealed the deal. They could see I was worried about Tammy. They could see her pain. It was the last thing Tammy wanted: to have anyone watch her suffer. Since it was a long day out at the track before the wedding, both Rachel and Rick decided they were going to head to the hotel after we finished dinner. "Tammy, do you want to ride with us back to the hotel?" Rick said. "I could use the break from all the hoopla."

Tammy turned to me, "You stay with Ashley?"

Since Ashley wasn't ready to leave I said, "Yes," bitten by the thought that Tammy gave in to the pain and relieved that she gave in to the pain all at the same time. "Me and Ashley. We're double trouble," I added, smiling. I kissed her forehead softly and whispered in her ear, "When you get back to the hotel, do you think you need to take the pain meds the doctors gave you?"

She resented the pain medication. She would say time

and time again, "I don't want to be loopy." I would say, "If you're hurting, you should take something," but it was a tricky trade-off. The pain meds rob you of quality time with the people you love. The high doses make you sleepy and you think, as you drift off into la la land that you're missing . . . everything. You lose a part of yourself along the way because the meds change you. It's like one day you're hoping to get a lot of things done or maybe go to the grocery store and all that seems like a big deal. The next day, just getting through each hour is a win and being the vibrant person you once were is a bonus. Tammy wanted to be present, no matter the self-sacrifice of pain.

She didn't respond to my suggestion. Instead, she made her way through the crowd, talking to everyone she knew. Hugs and smiles were handed out like candy at a parade. On Sunday, she came to the track. The van took her to the starting line where we were all scurrying about, getting Doug's car ready for his first-round race against Leah Pruett. Right after Doug won that round, the van brought her to the finish line to pick him up and then back to the pit area so we could get Doug's car ready for the second round. Dave Grubnic also won his first-round race, which meant two Kalitta cars moving on to the second round. Everything seemed to be going pretty smoothly.

In the second round, Grubby was racing a good friend of ours, Antron Brown. Pretty cool, he was the first African-American to win an NHRA Top Fuel dragster world championship, clinching the title the previous year. At that point in time, he had racked up thirty-seven Wallys, six of them the year before!

Ashley loved Antron. Everyone did. Racers aren't big guys and Antron was no exception. He was both slender and muscular, all compressed into a five-foot-eight-inch frame. When he walked into a room, though, he filled it up with his huge smile and positive energy. He's the kind of guy who asks you how you're doing and cares about your answer. He's very spiritual, like he operates on another level that somehow is closer to heaven than the rest of us. While we were always cheering on our teammate Dave Grubnic to get the win no matter whom he raced, we always hope that the person in the other lane has a good, clean, safe run. Unfortunately Grubby smoked the tires early in the run and shut off, giving Antron the easy win, but just as Antron was crossing the finish line, his 10,000-pound horsepower engine exploded, sending Antron on a wild ride down the famed Pomona race track. Orange yellow flames licked his car as it crashed into the left guard wall before sliding into the right guardrail and ended up in the Pomona sand trap. The car was on its side. The NHRA Safety Safari got to Antron quickly and pulled him out of his mangled dragster. Once everyone saw that he wasn't hurt, it was a huge relief for everyone, but Ashley was still devastated. Ashley just loved Antron because he was always so nice to her and always made time for her whenever he saw her. Even though Tammy was in a lot of pain, the mother in her came out full throttle! She walked Ashley down to Antron's pit area so she could see that he was OK, and thank God, he was.

When we were all done racing, I knew Tammy was just plain done. We rode back and had a nice quiet meal at the hotel in Pomona. The following day, I accepted my friend Cowboy

Bob's offer of the Presidential Suite at Hilton's Waterfront Beach Resort in Huntington Beach, about thirty-five miles from Pomona. Tammy was so excited. But first, we had a fix to feed. The O trio stopped at In-N-Out Burger for lunch, home of the "animal burger." The place was packed, as usual. I love their double doubles: two patties and two slices of cheese (it's been a long time since I've had one of those). I read one guy ordered a 100-by-100 once. (More fun facts: famous chef Julia Child carried a list of In-N-Out Burger joints in her purse she loved them so much and, quite coincidentally for me, the restaurant's founder Harry Snyder owned 50 percent of the Irwindale Raceway, a California dragstrip.)

After we stuffed ourselves, we battled crazy Southern California traffic to get to our hotel. The short drive was a normal thing that normal people do on a trip. And all that normal made us all feel like the cancer was at bay, like we'd left it back in Ypsilanti. It felt good. We were happy.

Once we got to the Hilton, Tammy told me she needed a nap so we could do some sightseeing later. The weekend just wore her out. Thank you, Cowboy Bob. The room was decked out with chocolate-covered strawberries, Mountain Dew for Tammy, and Crown Royal Reserve for me. I opened all the windows to the suite. A flood of ocean air breezes filled the room, a perfect backdrop for Tammy as she got some much-needed rest. While Tammy napped, Ashley and I walked to downtown Huntington Beach to check out the sights. It was a good way for Ashley and me to spend some time together. Teenage girls are like butterflies when they shop. They touch everything and flit from one "I-have-to-have-this" top to the next "I-need-these" Vans shoes and then on to the next big thing. We wandered into a store that sold shirts with big type that said "FUCK CANCER" on them so I bought one for Tammy. Ashley and I didn't talk much about Tammy's condition. We didn't have to. We were there for each other, we were present, and that was understood. That mattered most.

Since we only had one night in Huntington Beach, we wanted to make it a good one. Tammy finally woke up from her nap, and we headed downstairs for a nice dinner that Cowboy Bob had set up for us. While we didn't raise all sorts of hell or carry on like little kids or even sightsee as a family because of Tammy's pain and fatigue, it was a great night. It was a quiet night, just the three of us. It felt like the cancer didn't join us for dinner. When we got back to the room, Tammy had a bite of a chocolate-covered strawberry and went to sleep. I left all of the doors to the outside open so we could hear the ocean, and we did. It went whooshhhh over and over again, like a lullaby for Tammy to relax to. I liked hearing the sounds of something larger than us, larger than the cancer, larger than all the lousy facts and medical jargon and pain.

There's a peace in getting lost in that kind of no-holds-barred wonder.

*** 

The next morning I knew it was time to say goodbye to my girls and take them back to LAX so they could fly home.

I went as far as non-passengers could go, my hands stuffed in my pockets, and watched them walk through security. Tammy looked back over her shoulder. I smiled, blew her a kiss. Then, like the surging drum of the ocean waves we'd heard the previous night biting into the shoreline, the significance of the Pomona trip suddenly washed over me. It all made sense now. Why she wanted to come here so badly. Why she pushed to make it happen, defying the doctor. Why she convinced me that her traveling was no big deal. Why she visited with so many, many people. She wanted to say goodbye to her racing family. She knew the first race of the season was the last race she could travel to. All at once, the things we would never do flickered in my mind. She always wanted to see Niagara Falls. We'd never do that now. We talked about someday renewing our vows and walking the beach when we retired and traveling to all sorts of places. My heart started racing and the voice on the loudspeaker was louder than it should have been. There were too many happy people in that damn airport.

I missed her. Her getting on that plane left me vacant, especially after all the fun we had. I know she felt the same way.

I continued on to Phoenix for the next race. I was going through the motions. I knew my job. I loved my job. But I loved Tammy more. And, somehow, in a crazy, innocent, strange way, it seemed like that one fact gave me more happiness than I ever had taking home a Wally.

The cancer was consuming Tammy in places that were causing great pain. We were trying to do everything we could to manage it, but you could tell she was getting sicker. Once she got home, things got really bad and Dr. Stella considered Tammy's pain medication, making adjustments.

When I returned from Phoenix a week later, I thought

*I'm finally doing something right.* I felt good about doing things for Tammy and putting her at the center of my world. She was always way more organized than me so it wasn't like I could just take over and plan elegant dinners or clean the house the way it should have been cleaned. Tammy and I were a part of each other's lives again fully and without apology, though. Being there with her was more important to me than being successful in the eyes of others. There's a peace that comes from self-assuredness, a grounded happiness that sticks.

Taking her to the pain clinic or radiation treatments … these were times we spent together. We enjoyed ourselves, even as we struggled. Rest assured that, while we spent a lot of time going back and forth from the hospital, I still could piss her off just as much as when I spent a lot of time on the road. That was a good thing, too, because I liked seeing the strong fighter in her come out; it was part of who she was.

As each day went by, Tammy was getting more and more excited because she was close to coloring her hair again. She had to wait a certain amount of time after chemo had ended. She was counting the days down! We were on our way to Dr. Stella's office for her weekly visit with the hope of good news, too. The week before, Tammy had another PET scan done to see if the cancer was behaving and not spreading.

Now, Dr. Stella was the type of guy who didn't beat around the bush. He said Tammy needed to do spinal fusion surgery in her neck. The bone was deteriorating from the disease and they would have to literally fuse the vertebrae together (a very lame, layman's way of saying it) and insert metal implants. Bottom line:

They didn't want the spinal cord to compress causing paralysis, and they needed to do something to treat the chronic pain.

On Thursday, Dr. Stella and some of the other doctors from St. Joe's said it would probably be about a week or so before they could do the surgery, so I stuck with my plan to trade Michigan's late winter chill for Texas sunshine. The next day, I headed to the Mac Tools Fair since Tammy's younger sister Teri was up from Houston visiting for a week. The two were tight. Teri, the baby of the family, never shed her starring role as the "chosen one" shared by "babies" everywhere. Tammy was very protective of her sister, judged cuter and prettier than her older sibling during their years growing up in Ohio.

The Mac Tools Fair is where all of the Mac Tools distributors, dealers and executives gather in one spot and roll out new tools, programs and incentives that will hopefully be great for business. It's also a great way for many of us at Kalitta Motorsports to interact with the folks who sponsor our Top Fuel car. As the flight attendants from Delta started closing the door to the plane, Tammy called to tell me that the doctors were going to do the surgery on her neck the very next morning. Her voice, slightly higher than usual, sounded scared, but I also knew that she was hopeful the surgery would fix her pain. I was stunned and caught off guard that they had moved up the surgery. Trying not to cause any delays with the flight I was on, I continued on to Dallas. *I'll just catch another plane when I get there and head home,* I thought. Once we landed, all of the flights were sold out until the next morning. I couldn't believe it. I called Tammy to let her know that I wouldn't be able to get home until mid-morning, which meant I would miss her going into surgery. Of course, Tammy told me she would be fine because Teri was there with her, which just worried me more. I joked with both of them that there was always a sudden drop in IQ when they were together.

Tammy asked me to take a picture with Tony Merritt, who was the head of motorsports for Mac Tools. Both Tammy and her sister Teri looooooooved Tony. According to them, he was the best-looking man in motorsports: about five foot eleven inches with dark hair and a smooth, Southern Ohio accent. I just hoped I was second in Tammy's eyes!

I did end up getting that picture with Tony, said "hey" to a few people I knew, and caught a flight the next morning back to Michigan to be there when Tammy got out of surgery. When I entered her room, I wasn't fully prepared for the comedy routine that would follow. Both Tammy and her sister were as goofy as ever. You would have thought they were putting on an act for all the other patients at St. Joe's. Oh, yes, Tammy waved her iPhone, with the flashlight turned on, in the air and acted like she was sitting front row at a George Straight concert, cheering on her favorite country singer. I loved how she made it feel like we were all just hanging out. And then there was the Abbott and Costello-like routine. Tammy played the straight comic part. In a neck brace, she talked to Teri, who stood purposefully just outside Tammy's range of site. Since she couldn't move her neck to see to the right or left, Tammy bitched at Teri to move to a visible spot in front. Teri, playing the goofy comic part, thought the advantage was funny and stood to one of Tammy's sides where all Tammy could do was hear her sister's grating voice. Oh my Lord,

I'm sure there could be a movie made on those two; I just don't think there's an actress in the world who would want to play my sister-in-law.

Even though Tammy was in good hands, I felt as though I should have been there and not left for Dallas in the first place. But, like many things in life, what was done was done.

\*\*\*

The first day of spring had just come and gone. With winter's freeze behind us, the damp air smelled hopeful. I prayed like hell we would soon get a green light for Tammy to color her hair. I wanted that for her more than anything else I ever wanted for myself. The spinal fusion surgery was a detour. She had the color all picked out. It was going to be auburn.

And that's when we found out there were two cancer spots that had popped up on Tammy's brain. I was like: what!!!?!? Of course, this news deflated me. Tammy, on the other hand, wanted to know what needed to be done. Dr. Stella suggested radiation as soon as possible. One of the side effects would be that Tammy would lose her hair again. Tammy brushed her hand over the short bristles of her salt-and-pepper-colored crew cut and actually laughed out loud. "Damn," she said lightly, "I was so close to getting my hair colored again and then you had to tell me this . . . . oh well . . . I guess I better get some cool hats to wear since I'm gonna be bald again!"

I didn't take it so well. I wanted Tammy to color her damn hair. Because that's what she wanted. I hated how cancer was throwing his weight around, showing us who was boss. It hit me that Tammy was in real trouble. We didn't talk about her illness much and we were hopeful that Dr. Stella found the spots early enough so that we could head them off, but we also knew that maybe we couldn't. Tammy, by now, was used to hearing not-so-good news, so she put on a brave face and made it seem like no big deal. Of course, Tammy didn't want anybody to know. And she didn't want anybody to fret so she kept quiet about the news. But I knew it must have crushed her inside. As for me, I stuffed my disappointment way down deep inside like a child covers his eyes to make the boogeyman go away. I buried my fears so that the only time I saw them squarely in front of me was at night sometimes when I would dream about them.

On those nights, I would wake up and just want to cry.

## MIRROR IN SIN CITY

*Connie "The Bounty Hunter" Kalitta was the first driver to hit 200 mph in an NHRA-sanctioned event. When you look back at your own track record, the measurement you might consider is: "Did I do what I wanted to do?*

It was early April. Our next race was in the city that truly never sleeps, Tammy's favorite place to visit for a long weekend, Las Vegas. Without her with me on this trip, it was just another race. The track was located in the north end of town by Nellis Air Force Base where we would always get a free air show compliments of the U.S. Air Force. I never asked Doug if he would rather fly one of those planes than drive our race car. Knowing Doug, he would have wanted to do both.

After flying into Vegas on Thursday, I met up with Cowboy Bob, Nicky and Jon O at a cool hot rod shop where Cowboy Bob kept some of his old hot rods. A glint of light ricocheted off the whiskey bottle. The shop was fully stocked with parts, cars and a full bar. In the back of my mind, I was thinking about Tammy, about how we were just two scared kids getting married in that city a couple decades earlier. For a moment, time jogged backward. In my mind, I could feel the warmth of a Las Vegas sun. Suitcases tossed on the bed. The boardwalk, the chapel, the fake plants, the smell of broiled fish from the Japanese restaurant, the dorky clothes, the first kiss as Mr. and Mrs. James Oberhofer, the last kiss before we drifted off to sleep in each other's arms that night. The past. All those years in between. I wanted them back.

I thought about the years since then. Regret started biting me in the ass. I washed down the sadness, the fear of losing Tammy with one glass after another filled with the smooth, caramel-colored liquid. I started feeling sorry for myself is what happened. I was with my buddies. They understood me. It felt good. It felt so good running further and further away from the truth.

My wife was home sick. She had no escape from the pain or the cancer. She was suffering. Alone. And so was I.

When I got back to the hotel, I walked toward the heavy glass front doors, catching the bar across the street in the corner of my eye. I stopped, turned and stumbled over the curb. I pushed open the black, swinging door too hard. The sound inside washed over me, a jumble of tones like instruments warming up before a concert. Ice cubes clinked against glass, people were laughing and the voices slashed through me like knives being tossed about the room. A silvery laugh came from a girl at the bar. Someone brushed past me; I must have been standing there a bit too long. It was a bad moment. I knew this wasn't a good thing. I closed my eyes, but couldn't block out the shame. I had already crossed the line. I grieved for the inevitable. I set aside the fact that I still had more time with Tammy. That it wasn't over. I loved her. But I wanted more time, more days. Why was I here? Guilt tugged at me as I asked the bartender for a Crown and Diet Coke. Losing. Losing. Lose her. I was losing her. I didn't want to face the truth. I wanted distance between me and the truth.

I submitted myself to the smooth flow of Crown as it washed over me, disengaging me from emotional pain and making me feel invincible.

The next day, a massive hangover clobbered my brain. It was a stupid thing to do. Drinking doesn't do anybody any good, especially when you're trampling through self-pity.

So, let me ask a guy question straight-up: are many of us just a few shades off from being an alcoholic?

Oh, sure, I know there are men who don't drink. God bless you. The rest of us, it seems, have a relationship with some type of elixir, and that relationship is predicated on what the hell is going on in our lives. Now, to be clear, I'll never give up drinking (a personal thank you to Canadians for producing what I've long considered a coveted national treasure, Crown Royal), but drowning in it isn't smart either.

You see, when I was caught up in winning and was more crew chief than husband-father, Crown was the river to fun times, letting go, taking a little side trip from the pressures of life. Did I drink too much? Probably. I never thought of myself as drinking too much. Sure, I probably could have dropped in at an AA meeting, plopped myself in a chair, sat in the circle, and felt right at home sharing my life story. At the end of the day, though, I always felt like I had things under control. Besides, I figured having one vice wasn't all that bad compared to a lot of other guys out there. My Las Vegas binge, a mistake I would not repeat again, showed me how drinking until you're so fucked up you can't say a complete sentence is just plain stupid.

It was like a mirror reflecting exactly who I used to be. And, with that image, I also saw the man I had become.

# THE PROMISE

*Spark plug electrodes are totally consumed during a Top Fuel pass. It's like when you make a promise: you're either are all in or you're not.*

The house got pretty quiet after I returned home from Vegas that first week of April. As the cancer spread to Tammy's brain, she experienced severe headaches and a lot of pressure behind her eyes as well as in other parts of her body. As the rains showered down, she began spending more and more time in the hospital than at home. My Kalitta Motorsports office was now temporarily moved to whatever hospital room Tammy was in at the time. The average routine went like this: I'd get up in the morning, check in with Ashley, and go to St. Joe's where Tammy worked to get the pain under control.

Tammy lay in a hospital bed, monitors all around her, asking again and again when she could leave; she wanted out of that hospital like nothin' else. But because the cancer had spread to Tammy's bones, the treatment was changing.

Ashley's graduation on May 31 was six weeks away.

Now, getting dressed was a point on the board. Walking, another point. There was shortness of breath and a quiet, underlying anxiety about the road ahead. And, more and more, there was pain. The worst part was her voice though. Her once strong, silvery voice grew more and more quiet. It was thinning, like a thick, white chalk line slowly narrowing on a long blackboard. Still, she had that beautiful sparkle in her eyes that reminded me of the day she walked into Kalitta Motorsports fistfuls of years before.

The sun tried to peak out from behind gray clouds the day she and I and Dr. Stella decided the pain was skidding out of control. We couldn't get traction on this anymore. The cancer had spread to her spine; it was in her brain and kidneys. Our crew at St. Joe's wanted to do radiation on spots in her neck and spine. But the radiation could not be performed because Tammy was in too much pain to lie on the radiation table. In fact, Tammy was drowning in constant, chronic pain, especially when she moved. Pain was as much the enemy as the cancer now and even more devious: it could be sharp or dull, intermittent or constant. We had to manage this monster. Dr. Stella and other doctors from St. Joe's suggested implanting a pain pump into Tammy that would constantly feed medication through her spine. It was the only hope we had to get control of the situation. Without the pump, Tammy's only weapon was heavy medication, which made her so out of it that she couldn't talk or function. That's why I had to make the decision about actually going through with the pain pump implant. To me, there was only one choice.

When Tammy woke up from the procedure, she was furious.

"What is this thing in my side?" she pitched desperately. "Who did this?!?!"

"It's a pain pump to feed pain medication right to your spine," I explained calmly. I was sitting in a chair next to her bed. It was just me and her in the room. "It will help you out with the pain tremendously."

"I don't need this thing ... get it out of me! Now!!" I never thought I'd be happy to see Tammy's rebellious side come out, but there it was. Had she given in, had she shrugged her shoulders in defeat, I think my heart would have broken right then and there.

"Look, I understand. I know it sucks that you didn't make this decision, and it happened while you were out of it. I get it. But it's a good thing. You're going to feel better. You're going to feel less pain. And once the pump starts working, you're going to be able to get out of this hospital for good. And spend more time with me. With Ashley. It's a good thing, honest." I'm not sure where the words came from, but I wanted her to know that everything I was doing, and would ever do, would be in her best interest.

She was kind of quiet. I could see she was chewing on what I said. So, I decided some humor might help her turn the full corner. "You've got a better pump in you than we've got on our race car."

I probably went a little too far with that one.

***

With the fight against cancer in full swing, Tammy stopped going into the office so she was stuck with me much more than before. It was her and me against the world now. She would make a pretty good case about why she needed to go in and do some work, but I knew it was hard physically. "I have so much catch-up to do," she would complain. So, I came up with a brilliant idea to keep her connected.

We'd go to the pain clinic now two or three times a week. I would gauge how she was doing and text Rachel or Chrissy back at the office and ask them to meet us for lunch. We'd be driving back from the hospital, and I'd ask Tammy, "Are you hungry?"

"No, not really," she would answer quietly. She was wearing one of the West Coast Choppers hats given to her by our really close friend Jesse James, famous for having married Sandra Bullock and for making the best motorcycles on the planet. West Coast Choppers was his branded clothing line that often features the symbol for choppers everywhere: an iron cross—originally an emblem for bravery and heroism—with four points that arc wide at the ends. It was the right hat for Tammy to wear because she was courageous in my eyes, plus beautiful to boot. (The one and only wig she ever bought was stuffed in a dresser drawer, never used. I'm guessing it made her feel like someone else, like it was a disguise.)

"Well, let's stop anyway. Just for a bite." Then we'd go in whatever restaurant it was and there'd be all the girls from the office and everybody would act so surprised that Tammy was there. As the cancer consumed her more, she didn't want people to see her make the "pain" faces. Walking or standing up straight wasn't easy, but I knew seeing people who loved her and who she loved was important. I would tell her that she was just as beautiful as the first time I met her, it was just in a different way. I saw "who" she was, now, not just what she looked like on the outside. Those "surprise" lunches brought so much joy to the girls and to Tammy. I felt like I was in seventh heaven.

After three or four of these impromptu visits, Tammy figured out the get-togethers weren't by chance. By then, we'd pull out of the hospital and I'd be motoring up the road, asking, "Are you hungry?"

And she'd say, "Who's going to be there?"

I just laughed. That's all I could do . . . just laugh.

\*\*\*

Love. All roads lead to love—even for crotchety old guys who make most people piss in their pants. Tammy ran the accounting department for Connie's race team and as she came in less and less, she was hell bent on resigning. Tammy would never take something that wasn't hers. Her values and work ethic wouldn't allow it. Brutally honest and naturally antagonistic, Connie refused to listen. He told the girls back in the office, "Keep her on the payroll. You don't abandon people like that, especially someone who has done so much for this company."

You see, everybody banded together. Connie, the people at Kalitta, people I knew in the racing business, friends . . . Tammy's illness brought out many good things in many people.

Like Bob Lawson, from our office at Kalitta Motorsports. He lost his father and his sister, and then later on he lost his mother, so he would talk to me about next steps, giving me heartfelt advice. He told me to enjoy whatever time I had with Tammy and to make the best of it all. He gave me advice on how to be more efficient so I could spend less time at the office and more time at home. Of course, he always knew me as an eighty-hour-a-week guy. It wasn't a label I was proud of anymore. And he knew I wished that I had been more involved earlier when Tammy first got the news of her cancer. He felt my guilt. Now that I spent most of my time—outside of the actual races—working from home and hospital rooms, he was trying to tell me that forgiving myself would help me heal and even help me enjoy my life more. With a slight build and short hair, he always smiled because he genuinely looked at the bright side of life. He tried putting things in perspective for me.

"We all have business and distractions in life," he told me one day in a really kind voice, "where we don't listen and retain everything or put forth all of our energy at the right time. Sometimes, it takes a little bit longer . . . " He adjusted his metal-framed glasses and ended the conversation by looking at me straight in the eye and saying, "I don't know if what I said helped."

It really did help. It really did.

*\*\**

At work, not a lot of people knew the gritty details of Tammy's day-in-day-out fight with cancer, largely because Tammy never wanted to place her burdens on others. And she hated having anyone see her suffer. The Kalitta team did, however, know when it got worse. One hint was Tammy's fierce insistence she be taken off the payroll.

It was early May and Tammy asked me to take her up to Connie's office. She was going to march into his office and resign. "Call Kathy E right now," she insisted, "and find out when I can see him." She was serious.

I called. There just aren't a lot of choices when the woman you love is giving you marching orders like a four-star Army general. "Hey Kathy, Jim O here," I said, hoping like hell that Connie was out. "Is the boss man available today? …Tammy wants to see Connie." The thought of her walking in there made me queasy.

Fortunately for everyone involved, Connie has a booming air cargo business, Kalitta Air. "He's in Afghanistan for the week on business," Kathy explained.

"Well, you can't see him today," I told Tammy as I pressed the little red circle to end the call on my cell phone, relieved, "because he's in Afghanistan for the week."

"Really? Well I don't want to go to Afghanistan right now!" she answered, her voice edged in sarcasm and disbelief.

"OK," I said, "Thank God!"

To be honest, I was really thanking the Big Guy for putting

Connie halfway around the world and out of reach from a woman hell bent on a mission to resign.

*\*\*\**

A few days later, we were on our way to St. Joe's when Tammy asked me a question that I think most people who have a serious illness wonder about. She said, "Why do you think I got this?" My eyes were steady on the road. The tires went round and round in a quiet, rhythmic thump . . . thump . . . thump.

She continued, "I mean I would think a bad person would get punished with something as hard and awful as this."

"I think you saved our daughter's life," was all I said. And it was true because there was once upon a time when our daughter charged down the wrong road. Now, she was on the right one. Part of it was maturity. Part of it was our love. And part of it was the wake-up call Tammy's cancer gave each of us.

"OK, I'm good with that," she said without hesitation.

It was the only time she ever questioned the cancer. She didn't even challenge my answer. She had made her peace.

*\*\*\**

Look, let me just say this right here. You have to know that happiness means seeing every day as a gift. OK, how many fucking psychiatrists and spiritual gurus say that? I know, trust me, at first pass it's nothing new or earth shattering. BUT IT IS BECAUSE IT'S TRUE AND FEW OF US REALIZE IT. You either embrace life or you run from it or you don't know how to deal with it so you drink or do stupid stuff like that. Every one of our decisions puts us on a different path in life. Some of those paths put distance between us and happiness, some deliver it to our doorstep. Bob Lawson said once that making those decisions really shows who you are. He was right about that.

Everybody at Kalitta stepped up when Tammy got sick. Knowing I had the right people in the right places helped me keep my priorities straight and loosen the reins a bit and gave me the confidence I needed to be who I wanted to be. If you asked anybody at the shop if they could have done more to help Tammy at that time, everybody would say "yes," but that's not how she wanted to play her cards. The less they saw of me, the more they could see Tammy was getting worse. I wasn't at the office as much, and I didn't always stay extra days at the track when we went on the road. Some phone calls, emails and meetings took a backseat. Our cars were running well, but we weren't winning and that's just the way it was. I cringed at the thought winning ever defined who I was or dictated how my day turned out.

***

Once again, even though the issues we were dealing with were as heavy as a 426 Hemi engine, there were these little sparks of light, especially when the drugs made Tammy say the craziest things. We would laugh. Why? Because we decided happy was a better alternative to sad. Yep, there were these sweet, funny moments like Tammy calling me Jim Pisserhoffer Oberhofer while in the same breath talking about her "sweet" Ashley. There was also the time that Rachel came up to visit Tammy while I was there, and Tammy had us looking under her hospital bed for the little "kid" hiding. On occasion, she asked who the other patient was in the room—when there was just me and her in the room.

Through it all, graduation was the goal and we knew it. The

question then became: Can we maintain the cancer and the pain to get us there? We planned Ashley's high school graduation day with an urgency most parents couldn't imagine. I'd seen parents of Ashley's friends talk about how bittersweet this turning point was for them. No more proms. No more shoes to trip over in the hallway. No more plays or football games or award nights. We didn't have those concerns. We were just going to be happy to see it all together, the O trio.

Tammy was so excited about Ashley's graduation and wanted to do so many things to celebrate our baby girl, but the pain held her back. Things like sending out graduation announcements fell into my hands, and, luckily for me, I had Rachel help me get those done and sent out. Although petite in stature, she packed a punch when it came to personality. She showed up as a fearless supporter of both Tammy and me. She'd brush her dark bangs to the side, smile until her eyes crinkled and say, "Jim O, give me a job. Whatever extra hand you need." The support system we had was amazing to say the least!

Many of these people, in fact, came together to celebrate Ashley's May 14 birthday. Of course, May is THE month for celebrating motherhood. For Tammy and me, though, it was always the time each year we celebrated our daughter, who was born on Mother's Day. I had asked Ashley if it was all right if we invited people to the birthday bash, people who would like to see Tammy. Ashley was all thumbs up over the idea. We headed to our favorite Japanese Hibachi steakhouse called Ichiban. Close to forty people came. As usual, Tammy was a trooper and even though she was in a lot of pain throughout the evening, she gave everyone her time and attention. My sister-in-law Kim took a picture from that night that I treasure. Tammy is standing on one side of Ashley, wearing a blue jean ball cap with Las Vegas written out in sparkly sequins, and I'm on the other side. The picture shows us, like bookends, giving Ashley a big smooch on her cheeks. With her eyes closed, Ashley's adorable, round face is all scrunched up in a gigantic smile. I love that picture because we were all together and happy. It seemed like the celebration would just last forever.

That picture, to me, represents something Tammy had wanted from me for a very long time, something a mother who is very sick longs for in the father of her children.

She never asked it of me, but somehow I just knew. That's how love works.

Tammy wanted Ashley and me to be close. (Much later, Jon O would tell me Tammy had confided in Kim, his wife, that Tammy feared Ashley and I wouldn't share a close bond.) It was a simple and understandable hope for a mother who loved her daughter deeply. Tammy wanted me to fiercely watch over our Ashley and love her without condition or judgment—just like Tammy had loved the people in her life. In my more selfish days, I hadn't always done that, and it worried Tammy that I would fall back into old habits. But I kicked that guy to the curb, and there was no way I was inviting him back. In my heart, I made a promise to the mother of our only daughter that I would cherish our baby girl and watch over her and make sure no harm ever came to her. I couldn't say my promise to Tammy because I had racked up a lot of false starts and burnt out promises over the years. Nope. Words can't buy you a cup of coffee. This time, my actions would prove that I was the father she always knew I could be.

I had changed. And the big takeaway from that change for you, for me and for anyone who wants to be happy is this: we're all in this race together. Our pit crew is made up of the people we love. I missed that before, like I was living a life for one when I should have been living a life for three, five, ten, one hundred. We touch so many people. I don't think God made hearts to be small. I used to miss dinners at home even when I wasn't on the road. Forget that noise. I ignored Tammy's stress and loneliness. Not anymore.

In many ways, the journey I was now on snapped me to attention. And with that awakening, Tammy's unrelenting strength and courage throughout her battle with cancer reached me and saved me from myself.

# NIAGARA FALLS IN SPRING

*Before you reach the end of this sentence, a dragster can reach 300 mph. Some days go by just as fast.*

I came home from the Kansas Nationals in Topeka, not ready to fully face the entire crew assembled in my house. We had about two weeks until graduation. Tammy's sister had come to stay while I was gone. Whenever Teri was around, it was like having Gilda Radner's nutty character, Roseanne Roseannadanna, in the house: Teri was sometimes tactless and narrow-minded. But, I have to say, I was grateful for her too. Really grateful. We didn't need a parade of teary-eyed spectators, we needed soldiers holding us up. And Teri did that with both love and courage and humor.

At that point, Ashley had taken her mother's spot of running things, thank the good Lord, so she and Teri went around and ran errands and kept the wheels of the house moving. I walked into the bedroom and there they were, Ashley propped up against the headboard with pillows and Teri sitting on the end of the bed Indian style, while Tammy tried to find a comfortable position. I walked over to my girl and gave her a kiss. I sat on the edge of the bed (there wasn't much room left) and knew something was up. The three of them looked like little kids who had stolen cookies out of the cookie jar with Tammy being the ringleader.

"Are you going to tell your father what you did?" said Tammy, "Come on, just tell him." She was grinning.

Ashley inhaled deeply and grinned just as wide, "Do you want the good news or the bad news first, Pops?"

Sure, I'll play along. "Give me the good news first."

"I quit my job," she said smiling, her hands behind her head, chin held proudly high, like she'd been named CEO instead of ex-employee. My daughter held the strong belief that whatever her job, she wanted to make a difference, a hard thing to do while working for a big corporate logo. As proud as I was for knowing her desire to feel challenged and inspired, her waitress gig was still a paying job.

"That's the good news? What's the bad news?" I asked.

Tammy spoke first, "Just show him."

In Tammy's beautiful, elegant handwriting were the words "I love you, Mom" tattooed across Ashley's upper left ribcage like Tammy had written the note herself with one of those feathered calligraphy pens.

Ashley grinned, but her brow was tense. "You're not mad?"
Teri waved her ring finger in front of my face, showing off her tattoo. Really? The ring finger? Why bother?

"I love it," I said. Well, I did really love it because of what it said and the fact it was in Tammy's beautiful handwriting. I mean Ashley is my daughter and now she has permanent ink on her that wasn't there when we brought her home from the hospital eighteen years earlier, but . . . there are times when parents need to adapt. Today was my day.

The girls were all pretty proud of themselves. Now, the O's were connected in a new and different way.

I used to tell Tammy all the time I wanted to get a tattoo. She'd say, "Maybe your next wife will let you get one." Same thing with a motorcycle. To Tammy, though, Ashley could do no wrong. And, I have to admit, I felt pretty much the same way. Honestly, I trusted

Ashley and loved her so much that she could do just about anything, and I knew we would work through it. Grandma Hovenac's face suddenly appeared in my mind. I thought of all the times she felt the same way about me. I knew she was smiling down from heaven right then and there.

*** 

On May 21, a day when Tammy was feeling a little better than on other days, her oncologist, Dr. Stella, recommended hospice. Tammy stared at him, devastated. Hearing him say that word meant he had given up hope. He was our last line of defense. No more options. The pursuit of a miracle was over. We were benched.

We filed out in silence. There wasn't anything left to ask.

Tammy was upset for sure, but even more so, she was worried about Ashley. Tammy didn't want this burden to hurt the one person she loved more than anything else in the world. Even impending death is no match to a mother's love and her fierce desire to protect her child from the harshness and pain of this world. Tammy wanted Ashley to always feel as though everything would be OK, that life was good.

Of course, Ashley and I knew this was coming down (we had been told a couple weeks earlier, but didn't want this negative news to stop Tammy's positive march toward graduation), but there's always a part of you that pushes back and defiantly says, "No, you do not exist." I mean you kind of know death is inevitable when they say the words "stage 4 metastatic lung cancer," but you push aside the stats and believe what you've always known, that the people you love will be there forever. You know the end is possible when you see the shortness of breath, the unforgivable pain, the difficulty in doing everyday tasks. I mean you know, you see it, but you don't ever REALLY know. And you're never prepared when it shows up, rearing its ugly head screaming, "I'm here. I told you I would be here sooner or later."

Tammy, Ashley and I just left the news in the doctor's office and climbed into the truck. Before that visit, we were always on Tammy to beat the cancer, to eat right, to think positively. Now, cancer was in her brain, her spine, different organs. The doctors just told us we lost the fucking race. They used the "h" word. Then they went home to their families for a nice dinner. We wandered down the road like tourists lost in a strange city. Everything looked different. Tammy, of course, took charge. Thank God.

"I want to go to Taco Bell, and I don't want to hear a thing about it," said Tammy in a flat, pissed off voice. She got a Mountain Dew Baja Blast, a taco with ground beef and cheese only, and churros, a kind of Mexican fritter that's really just fried dough snowed on with lots of white powdered sugar. We got home, but being home wasn't the right place for us that night because homes are sanctuaries and ours felt upside down.

"Can we go to Target?" Tammy asked. I would have figured out how to get to the moon had she asked. "I want to get some new bath towels," she continued. "These things don't fit around my body right anymore." Before that day, she was very reluctant about a wheelchair. But I knew walking would be too much for her.

"Do you want to use a wheelchair?" I asked. My gut was sore. The doctor's words had hit me harder than any mosh pit punch I'd ever felt.

"Yes," she answered without hesitation, her head held high.

The three O's climbed back into the truck and we headed to Target—or Tarjé—as the girls liked to call it. Tammy and Ashley went to the girl's section and hunted. Soon, every piece of clothing in that department would be touched and analyzed with Tammy and Ashley's built-in sensors that immediately reported a hundred reasons why the article in question was acceptable or horrible. It was amazing to watch.

I lingered in the men's section, not really knowing where I was going or what I was looking at. A young kid asked me if I needed help. I looked at him and thought, *man, you have no idea.* Suddenly, an alarm went off inside me, and I thought I had better go find the girls. Honestly, I'm not sure how much time passed. By the looks of it, it was a couple carts full of time.

A pile of clothes the size of a pitcher's mound filled the basket. I must have been staring at it too long. I'd never seen a shopping cart so full. My mind was working out why we needed all this stuff. Tammy interpreted it as judging. "Maybe I should bring these back," she said, smoothing out the material of a blue shirt lying on top. She loved blue. "Maybe I won't need them anyway," she said quietly, more to herself than to me. *Or maybe there's a miracle around the corner,* I thought. *Or maybe I could just hold on to this moment, under these awful glaring lights and bad overhead music and figure out how to make it all last forever. That would be OK, too.*

"Everything is perfect," I said, tearing my eyes away from the cart and watching her now as she continued to grow the pile. "I love all of it," as my hand did a quick wave over the cart, like I was the Pope giving a blessing.

We found our way to the bath towels. I held up a big one to

show her. I like big.

"I don't like the colors of those towels," she said. She picked out smaller ones. After having a comical argument about how ugly the towels were that I picked out . . . we got both kinds. Three shopping carts full of shit later, we plunked down over seven hundred dollars. Who says you can't buy happiness? Well, you can—for a little while anyway.

We got back home and sorted through all the stuff and put everything away and Tammy started making fun of me because of my towels and I then made fun of her towels. And then I told her straight-up: we're going to Niagara Falls. I told her I didn't care if it took ten days to get there, we were going to do it. She started to fuss and, then, she just looked at me, shook her head and smiled.

Tough to argue with your best friend when they've made up their mind. I was never more sure of anything in my life because I loved Tammy and I wanted her to be happy. We were going on a road trip.

***

Later that night...

"I don't want to die," said Tammy.

"You're not," I lied. We were in bed when the big fat elephant in the room showed his big fat ass. It was time to talk. I knew this subject was coming—it had to—but I didn't want to talk about it. I wanted to push it far away the same way I wanted to pull the covers over my head right then and there. I never admitted that she was dying for fear it would make it come true. I wanted Tammy to be positive, and I didn't want to talk about endings. But, it wasn't about me. And I got that. Images flashed across the television; a man in a

TOP FUEL FOR LIFE

suit went on and on about something. The glare made us look blue.

"Ashley's going to be fine. You've done an awesome job with her. She's a lot. Like. You." I turned on my side, looked at her and sighed. The sheets made a crinkly sound. I took what I was about to say slowly. "And I'll always be close to her to remind her of that," I said, my eyes taking her in with great love and tenderness. In that moment, I felt Tammy looked as beautiful as ever. Beauty was something the damn cancer just couldn't take away from her. She had no hair and could hardly stand, but I never looked at her in any way else but purely and wholly beautiful, like the stars or a great work of art. No matter what else is happening, these simple, innocent things make a person stop and feel a sense of wonder. That's how it was when I looked at Tammy, too.

She smiled. She didn't want my sympathy. She didn't even want my protection. She wanted my assurance that I would be there for Ashley. Now, I had made my promise. Under the soft glow of the television, the lines on Tammy's face softened. She closed her eyes and rested.

It was a good night after all. Finally, after all these years, I had given Tammy the one thing she always wanted. My promise that I would fiercely love and protect our daughter.

***

For almost as long as we were married, Niagara Falls topped Tammy's bucket list. We procrastinated and never went. The day after I told her about the trip, I found a medical supply place and got her a wheelchair. We only had a couple of days to plan the trip from the time it popped into my head. *Wheelchair, pain medication, medical notes, blue and purple tie-dyed blanket,* check. *Tammy's favorite badass beanie, insurance card, oncologist's phone number, black-and-white flannel zip up, luggage, Mountain Dew,* check. Tammy, Ashley and I climbed into Tammy's CRV and headed east. Since Ashley didn't have a passport, we drove through Michigan, Ohio, Pennsylvania and New York instead of Canada. We didn't have the luxury of time for things like passports. I was determined: We were going to do this if I had to push Tammy's wheelchair every mile to that famous waterfall.

The first night we stopped in Cleveland. Tammy struggled sleeping because of the pain, so I did too. I was constantly monitoring the time so I could tell Tammy when to push the button for her pain pump and when to take her medication. We made it to Niagara Falls the next day. The wheelchair was tricky in places where there were only steps or where it was steep, but she soldiered on. I pushed her for what seemed like a hundred miles in that chair, in front of some pretty rude tourists and tricky paths. Ashley, all smiles, followed wearing her bright green windbreaker. We snapped pictures along the way. Tammy was filled with excitement to see the sheer majesty of Niagara Falls. She wore the red West Coast Choppers beanie that Jesse sent to protect her bald head from the cold. She really looked like a badass wearing that beanie! I never felt she was any less beautiful than the day I first met her. Her eyes, filled with light, just took over whenever I looked at her. After our long trek, we stayed the night.

The next morning, I asked her, "Do you want to go back?"

"No, not really," she said, "I wasn't that impressed. Let's go to the mall and buy Ashley a graduation dress instead."

I couldn't believe Tammy wasn't impressed. You mean after all the times she and I talked about going to see Niagara Falls, she's not impressed? Holy shit! But, then, I realized that being a mother meant more to Tammy than any natural wonder of the world.

So, Tammy and Ashley shopped. The Target escapade came back to me, and I wondered in the back of my mind if I could really afford whatever pile the girls were going to make today when Tammy told me to stop the wheelchair so she could look at this red purse that caught her eye. She turned to me, looked me straight in the eye and said flatly, "I really want to buy this purse, but maybe I shouldn't because I won't be here." She asked it differently this time, like it was more matter of fact. I blinked. Not being the swiftest thinker in the room, I looked at her and told her to get whatever she wanted. My head, though, was shouting: *We can't possibly be done with this fight.* The purse comment showed Tammy's hand. She was accepting death. I didn't like that. It felt wrong. I wanted her to fight it, fight it with me, fight something, even though the doctor had recommended hospice, even though logic said the end was near. I didn't want to accept the verdict.

At this point, Ashley and I were bickering. The day was unraveling as it often does for people who love each other while being bombarded by life's fucking arrows.

"I want ice cream. Let's find ice cream," said Tammy in a this-is-what-we're-going-to-do-next tone. The wheelchair practically did a Funny Car burnout over to the Haagen-Dazs right around the corner.

"What kind do you want? Do you want to try some first?" I asked. We were off the purse subject, and I was pretty happy about that.

"I'm not sure, maybe vanilla or cookies and cream," she said.

The girl behind the counter gave Tammy a small sample of each and then Tammy decided, "Cookies and cream please!"

"In a cone or cup?"

"In a cup, one scoop, with a spoon," she said.

I went to pay, and the girl behind the counter looked at me and said, "This is on me," as she handed me the ice cream slowly, her eyes soft and kind.

Tammy sat there eating the ice cream, pain-free, happy, at peace for a full fifteen minutes. I'm like: Holy shit, we've been on her about her diet, taking pills, going to treatment and even had a pain pump implanted in her body, and none of those things made her happy or pain-free. They're not the real things that stick around. Like in racing. The thrill from winning trophies is short-lived. Sure, they give you a false sense of being happy, a temporary sense of being happy, like the cart full of shit at Target. But, there she was, smiling, enjoying life, feeling happy. It hit me that happiness grows by enjoying the simple things in life and loving the people around you.

At that point, I realized what I had been missing for years. Tammy had been sick for twelve months prior to our trip. Our lives could have been so much better if I had just taken the time to understand her. Sometimes, I would get defensive about things, not realizing she was having a bad day or needed a friend to listen. When she ate that ice cream, though, it all made sense. We were enjoying life. We were tasting life. The ice cream symbolized what could be spread over many days. It was losing ourselves in just being together and doing something fun, not ramming selfish expectations down each other's throats. From that point on, I decided the pursuit of happiness was the one true win. Others don't give it to you. Things don't give it to you. You create happiness and make it your own.

I thought back to Grandma Hovenac and the angel pins. Pray, she would tell me. I understand now. You're either bitter or you grasp on to your faith like crazy. I chose faith. I believed and trusted in God. In fact, I saw his hand in, of all things, ice cream.

Kids get the whole happiness concept. Have you ever seen a five-year-old hold up their hand and pass on an extra cookie? Hell, no. Kids demand happiness every time they open their mouths. I'll tell you what, somewhere along the line, people grow up and lose that grab-the-joy determination. We settle.

Ashley understood happiness better than I did. She embraced positivity and barred the door to anyone who even hinted at crying in front of Tammy.

You have to create a culture of happiness with love at the center. That's what ice cream and Tammy taught me at Niagara Falls. Our trip was one of the most difficult things I've ever done. There were many obstacles starting with our doctor thinking we were insane right down to the cancer's tentacles wrapping themselves around Tammy's body in painful, invasive ways.

But, we did it. And it was right. Because when you love somebody, you should risk everything you have to make dreams come true. Even if the big, old waterfall isn't that impressive. Even if you just end up shopping at the mall. Even if the journey is long and hard. The important part is that you were there and you cared and you did something big for the right reasons.

I felt joy.

\*\*\*

One day, soon after we got back from Niagara Falls, I was thinking about when I first met Tammy. I always told her that I loved her green eyes.

She found that odd. She was very self-conscious about her eyes and, over her lifetime, had had several operations on them. She had inherited a condition from her father that made one eye look a little droopy. When you start taking people for granted, you don't really see how or why they feel a certain way. You think, oh, it's just so-and-so, they just want to bitch about everything.

In the months since New Year's Eve, I looked at Tammy differently. I loved her eyes and everything about them, just as I did when we were first married. As she struggled with her appearance, as she lost her hair from the treatments and her pride from being less mobile, she was still that beautiful girl I met back in 1989. I didn't see a difference. I felt she was still the same.

Tammy was never flamboyant or over-the-top with things. She had a pure and simple beauty about her. No flash. The significance of that came back to me. She was always so polite, no matter what. She was a lady. If she had to dress up and go to a formal function, she could be just as much of a lady as anybody else. She could tell a joke, talk shit when she needed to talk shit and skewer the biggest ego in the room with her quick wit. Her heart was huge. She never put herself in front of anything or anybody.

I had the biggest crush on Tammy Ferrell. There it was, the sheer beauty of her, her pure and open spirit, her laugh that made me want to say funny things just to see her laugh again.

Days passed until, finally, we found ourselves on the night before Ashley's graduation day. I put my head down on the pillow.

I felt happy to lie next to the woman who had stolen my heart and, lucky for me, had always stubbornly refused to give it back.

*\*\**

The sun came up and shined its light the next morning. We made it to graduation day.

Our team was racing at Raceway Park in Englishtown, the same track where we had lost Scott. It was a Friday, and the first time I had ever missed a day of racing. Ashley wore a black-and-white dress we had bought her at the mall by Niagara Falls. She looked so grown-up that it made my heart stop for a minute. How far we'd all come. I pushed Tammy's wheelchair as we, along with her parents and her brother Tim and his wife Therese, made our way through the thick crowd in the gym at Eastern Michigan University where Ashley's high school held its graduation. It was a sea of several thousand people seated in the stands bordering the patch of excited graduates. When they called Ashley's name, Tammy put every bit of strength she had behind a big whoop of a cheer. I was the proudest I'd ever been of Ashley and Tammy. It was a surreal moment. That night beat out any race I'd ever been to.

A few months earlier, I had asked Ashley if she wanted to have a big graduation party. Ashley thought about it and had said, "I would, but I would rather have it at Englishtown on Saturday night during Eddie's Lobsterfest. I feel like my family is out at the track!" Eddie's Lobsterfest is a party we throw each year in honor of Scott. We used to call Scott "Eddie" when he had a few too many Coors Lights in him because he looked like Eddie Munster from the old TV show *The Munsters*. I thought it was a great idea, and so did Tammy.

With Tammy's parents keeping a good eye on their daughter, Ashley and I flew to LaGuardia Airport in New York City early on Saturday morning and then drove down to Englishtown. For the first time since Scott's accident, I actually looked forward to going to Englishtown, and it was because of Ashley!

Tammy told me every single time before a race: "You and Doug need to bring home a Wally." In Englishtown, we were on a mission to bring Tammy home a win. But, sometimes, when you try too hard, it just doesn't work. We lost to Brittany Force in the first-round eliminations on Sunday.

Let it go, I told myself. A race. Cars. Wins. Losses. Let it all go.

Even with the first-round loss, I was very proud of our team. Doug, Troy, Mac Savage, our clutch specialist, and the rest of the team did a great job running the car on Friday qualifying in my absence, which made me even more confident about our team. Without all of the great people at Kalitta, I wouldn't have been able to spend so much time with Tammy and Ashley when they needed me most.

What I was going back home to meant everything. What I was leaving at the track was one race of many.

Before I flew back on Monday, Cowboy asked me if he could make a stop in Michigan on his way to Vegas and see Tammy. Now how can you say no to Cowboy Bob?! I met him at our house, and we walked in together. Tammy's parents were there and Tammy was in bed.

I beelined it to her and said, "Hey, how you doin'?"

"OK," she said, adding, "How are you and where's Ashley?"

"I'm good and Ashley is downstairs with your parents," I

answered proudly, smiling.

Tammy was happy we had gone to the race together. She was proud of me. I could see she was happy. "There's somebody here to see you," I smirked.

Tammy responded, "I don't want to see anyone right now, I'm tired and I look like shit!" She let go of a deep breath.

I said, "You might want to see who's here."

"Who is it?" Tammy blurted out. I had peaked her interest.

"It's Cowboy Bob!" I said proudly, like I was presenting the President of the United States.

"OK. Let me fix my hair (she had none)," she said saucily as she got up slowly and walked into the bathroom. She sprayed on some perfume and came downstairs wearing black yoga pants and a flowery, kind of flowy top. My eyes scanned her from head to toe; she looked like a million bucks! She was elated to see Cowboy Bob because they had a special bond. She respected his honesty and the cavalier way he lived his life, like each day was the last, best one of the bunch. Too, Tammy loved country music and Cowboy Bob was the epitome of a country gentleman in every way. He always treated her with deep respect and she, in return, gave him a special place in her heart. They just sat there on the steps going down to the sunken living room like two best friends scheming up plans in the far corner of the playground at recess.

I couldn't resist. "Oh you get all dolled up for Cowboy Bob, huh?" I said, pretending to be jealous. Tammy just looked at me and smiled.

"Hey, you have a hairdo like me now," he said and she laughed. That just egged him on. "Hey, together, we make a good ass, don't we?" and he put his hairless head next to hers. She laughed even harder. I could have hugged Cowboy Bob right then and there. She didn't want to see anybody when she got sick, but she always wanted to see Cowboy Bob.

Happiness. Checked.

\*\*\*

Tammy LOVED casinos. So, right after Cowboy Bob's visit, she asked me a question that did not at all surprise me. "How about if we go to the Greektown Casino in Detroit?"

"I'll take you down there. No problem," I said.

"OK, that's fine," she hesitated. "I just don't want you to go in with me. You always make me feel so rushed in the casino."

"We'll take Ashley and she and I will go to Fishbone's for dinner. That way you won't feel rushed. How about it?"

Tammy agreed and off we went. Before Tammy went into the casino, we sat in the Toyota Tundra pickup truck and talked about how this was all going to happen. I was really pushing to at least stay with her until she got inside.

"Just … can I please walk you in?"

"No," she said quickly. "I can do this on my own," she said, turning her head to look me straight in the eye. "I really want to do this by myself, Jim O." I respected Tammy's pride in wanting to walk in on her own. She felt good about her independence, and I would never rob her of feeling that sense of accomplishment. Because of the cancer, she had to depend on so many people. She hated that. In a way, this was the best thing for her.

"Fine," I sighed. "We'll meet back at the Greektown VIP parking garage, the very spot where I'm going to park the car."

Ashley and I watched Tammy, slightly hunched over, slowly walk into the casino. After making sure Tammy made it in safely, Ashley and I had dinner. Fishbone's was attached to the casino. Of course, the whole time we were eating, I was worried about Tammy. She would send me a text every now and then checking up on Ashley and me, wanting to know what we were eating. Tammy kept asking me how long she could play, and I would just tell her as long as she wanted. After a while Ashley and I went back to my truck and waited for Tammy to call and say she was ready. After not hearing from her for a while, I started texting. Nothing. Then I called her. No answer. My heart raced.

Since Ashley was only eighteen, I told her to wait in the truck so I could find Tammy. Too much time had passed since I'd last heard from her. I walked up and down rows lined with slot machines that burped up high-pitched dings and grinding gear noises. People were everywhere. I searched their faces for Tammy. I knew she couldn't have gone very far because she didn't move real fast.

Finally I got a call from her asking me where I was. I told her I was looking for her and asked her where she was. She told me that she was right where we agreed to meet. I ran back to where we were parked. Still, no Tammy.

Tammy called me again asking where I was, and of course I told her I was still looking for her. She told me again that she was waiting right where we agreed to meet. I got a little frustrated and went back in looking for other VIP parking areas. I finally walked out into the valet parking area and, low and behold, there was Tammy talking up a storm with the attendants. Tammy told me it was about time that I showed up! I just laughed and told her that I got lost. All I could do at that point was laugh with relief that I had found her.

A few days later, Tammy asked me if she could go back to Greektown, but instead of me taking her, could Jon O's wife Kim take her. I told her it was up to Kim. Tammy then told me that she had already texted Kim and that she was on her way over. She said she would have way more fun at the casino with Kim because Kim wouldn't rush her like I did! Tammy really dressed herself up the night they went . . . almost like it was a big night out on the town. It was amazing to see her, as sick as she was, gather the energy and spirit to go. She got around completely on her own that night. I've read that people who are nearing end of life hit a high point where they, all at once, have a burst of energy to get up and move around, almost like before they got sick. That's why none of us could have foreseen what would happen just one week later to the day. No, for this one night, she summoned a burst of energy that allowed her to do things the way she wanted to do them. One more time.

And from what I hear, the girls had a large time!

And because Tammy was happy, I was on cloud nine.

# 7 DAYS MAKE A WEEK

*A Kalitta mosh pit, where arms are swinging in sweet victory, is a place where pain and joy go hand in hand. Life goes that way too.*

Walk with me here. Because each of us lives seven straight days and then we all get to start over. Seven days make a week. And we choose how it all goes down. I want you to walk with me and see what I saw and take away from it something good . . .

## WEDNESDAY, JUNE 12

Earlier that day when we were making our daily stop into the St. Joe's Pain Clinic, we finally decided it was time to have hospice come to the house. I was worried that I couldn't help Tammy the right way anymore because the pain fits were becoming too frequent, and I just didn't want to do anything that would set her back.

After our trip to the hospital, I took Tammy up to the Kalitta shop to see the girls in the office. Tammy walked into the shop and saw Sarah right away at the reception desk, and then started making her way down the hall. She REFUSED to use a wheelchair. Up next, Patricia's office, then Rachel's and back to her office to see Chrissy, Shawn and Megan. She was on a mission to see her girls! They all gave her gentle hugs.

Tammy also decided to make lunch plans with all of them for the very next day as well. She was excited about her plans, and I was so happy for her excitement!

We finally made it back to the house so we would be there in time for Tammy's appointment with the hospice caregiver.

After I answered a few questions, the hospice nurse asked Tammy what year it was. She answered, "1998."

The cancer was blazing its way through her brain.

\*\*\*

Scott's wife Kathy had called me earlier in the week and asked how Tammy was doing. Even though she got the Kalitta name by marriage, she always fit into the strong bonds of the family perfectly, as though she'd been with the gang forever. The last time she ever saw Scott, he was healthy and probably wild-eyed about something! But when he crashed, I was the one who broke it to her over the phone. I flew down after that just to see how she and their two sons, Corey and Colin, were doing. I remember her saying, "I always knew if you ever called me from a race track, something was bound to be wrong. When I saw your number, I knew it."

So, it was no surprise that Kathy hopped on a flight from Tampa to see Tammy.

"Kathy's coming up to see you," I eagerly said to Tammy.

"Really? Tomorrow, we're going to have a girl's lunch at The Full House and Kathy needs to be there!" she said. The place served up juicy, sizzling hamburgers with grease that soaked right into the buns. They also had keno which Tammy loved playing even though it seemed like she never won. Tammy just loved going to The Full House.

"I'll tell Kathy to meet us at the shop at eleven," I said.

"Oh, I've got a doctor's appointment with Dr. Patel in the morning," she answered. Dr. Patel was her general doctor for ages. The woman was gentle and treated Tammy with great kindness. They cared about each other.

"What time?" I asked.

"9:00," she answered.

I never asked why she would be seeing Dr. Patel after being treated by her oncologist all this time. I didn't think of asking her that.

## THURSDAY, JUNE 13

If we thought Niagara Falls was a hard trip to make, it looked like a Sunday drive down a country road compared to our journey the day of the big lunch.

We got in the car. "What's the address again?" I had taken her to Dr. Patel's once before, but not recently. I knew it was in Saline, about twenty minutes away, but that's about it. Tammy played navigator instead and just started throwing out directions.

"Go right, now go left. Go to the end of this street and then turn," she said.

We ended up in a parking lot. Clearly, it was not Dr. Patel's office.

"I don't think," I said flatly, "that this is where her office is."

"I don't think so either," she answered back.

"Give me the address."

She called the doctor and left a message. "We're running behind," she said, like we were on the way to a friend's house for a Saturday night dinner. A couple seconds later, my phone rings. It's Teri, Tammy's sister. Oh happy day.

"Tammy just left me a message," she said anxiously, "thinking it was for Dr. Patel. She said, 'I'm running behind.' What does that mean? Is she OK, Jim O? Are you with her?" I'm on the phone with Teri and looking sideways at Tammy, trying to fit the pieces together. I was never a good detective. We were losing time. We had an important lunch date to get to, but we had to make this side trip. I just didn't know why. I let faith take over and motor us forward.

"Everything's fine. We'll talk later."

I clicked off from talking to Teri and looked up Dr. Patel's address on my phone, 720 Woodland Drive. Finally, we pulled in. It dawned on me that, since we had been seeing Dr. Stella, we had stopped needing Dr. Patel a long time ago. Unfortunately, we were past annual physicals and the common flu. I put the car in park.

"Tammy. Why are we here?" I asked her quietly.

"It's for a checkup." She said it plainly enough, like I should have known, but it was OK that I didn't.

We walked into the small lobby decorated with soft pinks and blues. Tammy was leading this dance. The woman behind the counter greeted Tammy with a friendly hello while checking her in and told us she would let Dr. Patel know we were here. Suddenly Dr. Patel appeared and opened the door to the hallway. She invited us in and led us to the second exam room on the left. There were no windows in this room, but for some reason it seemed like the sun was shining in. We sat down there and all the while Tammy talked about her cancer, talked about her sweet Ashley (thankfully, she didn't mention Jim Pisseroffer Oberhofer!). We sat there for about an hour and the two of them talked about a lot of things. I played wingman and watched, taking the scene in. Then, Dr. Patel removed her stethoscope from around her neck and placed it on Tammy's heart. She checked her breathing and took her pulse. Checked her blood pressure.

"You're all good," Dr. Patel said with a smile. They hugged for a full minute.

Then, we left. As we walked to the car, with the big lunch still ahead of us, I realized Tammy had made the appointment with Dr. Patel so she could thank her and say goodbye. That's how thoughtful Tammy was. She took her love to her people.

I learned something that day. When you are preparing for life, you do certain things. When you are preparing for death, you do certain things.

It was kind of hard to be peppy after that, I have to be honest. It took a lot of mind energy for me to see below the surface.

"Now," I said, breathing deep, "you've got your big lunch."

"I'm too tired," she said slowly. She wasn't sad. I could have handled sad. She was . . . accepting. Acceptance is harder than sad.

"Come ahhhhhhn," I returned, in my best Jersey voice. "You haven't seen Kathy in a couple years. All the girls will be there, and you're the one who set this all up."

She stared out the window. I just kept driving.

I felt better once we pulled into the Kalitta parking lot. Kathy immediately met Tammy out by the car and helped Tammy walk into the office. Tammy was very excited to see Kathy, and it showed. Tammy all of a sudden had this huge burst of energy and was ready for lunch and keno! We walked into the office and there they were: the tribe! Tammy walked into a mosh pit of gentle hugs and love. They were all there: Patricia, Chrissy, Megan, Shawn, Rachel and Kathy. They shot the shit for a while and then everybody scooped up purses, keys and phones and piled into Rachel's car to head over to The Full House restaurant.

Before they left, I made sure Tammy was all buckled in and ready for the short drive. I reached over and gave her a kiss and told her I loved her and to have a good lunch and win some money at keno. Tammy looked at me and asked, "Do you want to come with us to lunch?"

"Nope, this is a girl's thing. You'll have a better time without an ass like me around," I joked. She smiled. My heart sparked. I loved making her smile.

As much as I wanted to join them all for lunch, I also knew that I had to get to the Detroit Airport to make my flight to Bristol that afternoon for our next race.

Once Tammy made it to The Full House, she kept calling me, asking me questions. Like what she should have for lunch and what I was eating for lunch, what time was my flight and when she should take her medication. I knew she was in good hands, so I didn't really think anything of it. I knew exactly what she would order, too: a Mountain Dew and the signature quarter pounder king with cheese and French fries. Every time she ordered it, she'd say: "I'll have a king with cheese, pleeeeeease" with a big grin. It was just a silly thing that always gave us a laugh. I also knew she would buy twenty dollars worth of keno tickets and look at the monitors placed throughout The Full House hoping she would win a few bucks.

After lunch, Kathy came back with Tammy and Ashley to our house to continue visiting. I landed in Atlanta to connect for my flight to Bristol and immediately called Ashley.

"How's mom, sweetie?" I asked.

"Good. Me and Kathy are going to make dinner," Ashley said.

"OK, cool, what are you making?" I asked curiously because I always knew Kathy was a great cook.

"Some sort of pasta and vegetables," Ashley said with excitement. "It sounds like it will be really good."

"OK, awesome, sweetie. I'm getting on my plane for Bristol now and I'll call you once I land. I love you, sweetie, and tell your mom I love her too!"

"Got it, Pops, have a safe flight, and I love you too!"

Once I landed in Bristol, I had a voicemail from Ashley. Tammy's pain had taken a turn. I called her back.

Ashley said, "Pops, it's getting worse."

"Make sure your mom has hit the pain pump button and that she has taken her medication," I said, running my hand through my hair.

"I did Pops, and it doesn't seem to be helping," Ashley said with concern.

"OK, let me call hospice and see if we can get someone out to the house."

My words were thick and heavy. My heart felt the weight of them. I just didn't know what else to do because nothing was really helping Tammy now, and I didn't want Ashley to have deal with all of this by herself.

The hospice nurse came out to the house and did what she could to make Tammy more comfortable and it seemed to be working at the moment.

Kathy and Ashley finally finished making dinner after the nurse left, but Tammy didn't feel like eating and just wanted to rest.

Once I made it to my hotel in Bristol, I called Ashley to see how everything was going. "It's OK now, Pops. Mom is sleeping."

As I lay down on the bed, I kept thinking about what I could or should be doing. How can I get back home from Bristol? I couldn't sleep. I stared at the ceiling, thinking about how I should have just stayed home. The struggle inside me to be at our races, to not disappoint Connie and our team, to fulfill my responsibilities as a crew chief, collided with trying to figure out the right thing to do for Tammy. Part of me, too, just wanted to carry on like normal in the middle of chaos and hurt.

I prayed that Ashley would be strong enough to get through this. I prayed for Tammy.

Everything was out of my control. I felt like a car that had run out of gas on the side of the road, its tank as dry as dust.

## FRIDAY, JUNE 14

The next morning, Tammy's parents came up from Fairborn, Ohio, about a three-hour drive away, to help take care of Tammy.

I never asked Keith or Virginia how hard it was on them to see Tammy in this condition, basically watching their beautiful daughter being consumed by cancer. I couldn't have handled it as well as they did.

During the day, Ashley would keep me updated on Tammy's condition. The pain was getting worse, and it didn't seem like the normal stuff was doing the job anymore.

Tammy told me many times: "Do not let me die in this house. You can throw me out on the neighbor's lawn or roll me over to Mike and Scott's house, but don't let me go in our home." Her directive didn't stop there. She also didn't want to be taken by ambulance. By now, you've probably figured out that Tammy is pretty headstrong. I tried to figure out why she dug in her heels about the whole house thing, and here's what I came up with: She didn't want Ashley to live in a place where death visited. Our home, while not always perfect, was a happy place and death sucks. A mother protects her children. She takes the arrows. On this point, Tammy was doing exactly that. As for the ambulance, that was simple. Tammy didn't want to put attention on herself. Ever.

I was walking down the dragstrip at Bristol Dragway, checking the track out and deciding how we needed to tune Doug's car for our first qualifying run, but wondering how things were back at home when my phone rang. It was Ashley.

"Mom's not doing good, Pops. She is in a lot of pain and I can't talk to her right now. I don't know what to do." Pain was winning.

My heart dropped right there on the track. I knew I needed to help my baby girl, but I didn't know how.

"Let's call hospice sweetie and have them come out to the house. It's the only thing I know to do."

I stood there in the middle of the track as Funny Cars were getting ready to start qualifying.

Ashley made the call to hospice. The nurse came over to see what she could do to help make Tammy more comfortable. These were kind strangers, and they understood death. Yep, they came over and met with Tammy, asked her a few questions, talked to her parents. The nurse suggested that an ambulance needed to be called to transport Tammy to St. Joe's. Of course Tammy wanted no part of that. Mr. Ferrell then helped his daughter to his car.

I never asked him what he was thinking, but, as a father, I can only imagine. Maybe he remembered the softness of Tammy's small fingers when she was five or six, and how they would walk hand in hand to the park together. Or the things he once said to wipe away the sting from a skinned knee when she fell off her bike. Or maybe just the fact that he would have changed places with Tammy a dozen times over if he could. He didn't want her to be the first one to go.

That's the wrong order.

Doors slammed. Ignition roared. Tears were pushed down. And then, a father drove his daughter to the only place she could be that particular day, St. Joe's Hospital.

After Keith made it to the hospital with Tammy, I was on the phone with him getting updates and talking with Dr. Craig who was in charge and very familiar with Tammy's condition. The hope was to try and get Tammy's pain under control with IVs filled with pain medication along with turning the dosage up in her pain pump. I tried to keep my mind occupied by doing the only thing that I could at that time: tuning Doug's dragster.

I prayed that night that Tammy's pain would somehow subside. I couldn't sleep as I wanted to be with Tammy and Ashley in the worst way, but I didn't know how to get there or if I should leave: I didn't have a crystal ball telling me exactly what was going to happen next and when. Plus, Bristol is in the middle of NOWHERE. You can't just walk up to a ticket counter in Bristol and buy a ticket to Detroit. I didn't know what to do. I hoped that things would be better the next morning. I thought about renting a car and making the ten-hour drive, but I felt I wasn't in the right frame of mind to be making a trip like that by myself. My mind wasn't clear because there is no playbook that tells you the game plan when you are losing someone. I was also too proud to ask for help.

Maybe I should have. Maybe I should have done a lot of things. I guess I'll never know.

## SATURDAY, JUNE 15

We were at the Bristol Dragway when Dr. Craig called me early the next morning with an update. The pain pump dosage was maxed out and if they used any more pain medication, he said, Tammy risked having a massive heart attack. I would never do that to her. I couldn't intentionally give her more medication to fight off the pain only to have her heart explode. *Think clearly. Think,* I told myself. Honestly, I still didn't have it in my head that Tammy was dying, was going to die. Even after all these months, the parade of hospice people, the pain, the shortness of breath, the gradual decline that left her confused sometimes and weak other times. I still couldn't face it. Then, the doctor said something, much in the same way a friend would suggest you try out their great accountant, a guy who was always reliable and on time. Dr. Craig asked that we consider a twilight drug that helped terminally ill patients pass away peacefully. I was shocked. Honestly, I thought this was like all those other times that we'd hit a speed bump, but would get right back on the road. I thought: *This is it. I need to get home.*

I asked Dr. Craig if he could wait until I got to the hospital before they administered the twilight drug, I wanted to be there. He said they would wait.

I talked to Doug and Connie and explained what was going on and asked if Doug could fly me back to Ypsilanti so I could be with Tammy and Ashley. Of course both Doug and Connie were more than willing to do anything that I needed. I told Doug: "Let's make our two qualifying runs and then we will leave." Doug told me that whatever I wanted, he would do. After we finished qualifying, Doug and I flew back in Connie's King Air, an eight-seater plane. We landed and I drove straight to St. Joe's Hospital. I wore a wristband with the universal symbol for gamblers everywhere: 777. Jesse made them and passed them out at Bristol. Jesse's kindness was as abundant as the tattoos that covered him from head to toe. He had wanted to do something that kept Tammy with us while we raced, and these wristbands were perfect.

Once I walked in, it felt like I was running against the wind, like I couldn't get to her fast enough. A ventilator was helping Tammy breathe. She recognized that I was there, and I mumbled a thank you to the Big Guy for that. She was scared, the look in her eyes told me she was really, really scared. Dr. Craig (a dead ringer for a younger-looking Santa Claus) explained everything that needed to be done and that we couldn't wait any longer. She could have a massive heart attack at any moment. They gave her the twilight drug. I stayed at the hospital all night with Ashley, Tammy's parents, Tammy's brother Tim and his wife Therese and Jon O's wife Kim. I prayed so hard I figured even Grandma Hovenac was up there, nodding with approval.

## SUNDAY, JUNE 16

The next morning, Dr. Craig explained that things were stable and that they would probably stay that way for a while. I met Doug up at Willow Run Airport and we took off on one of its four runways by eight the next morning. It was Father's Day and Ashley was by my side. I had a lot of races under my belt, but this one was different because Ashley was by my side. We were doing it together. It was exactly what Tammy had always hoped for. I had kept my promise. I thought to myself: I would figure out a way for Ashley and me to keep Team O going.

Race day in Bristol didn't go as well as we would have hoped, but that was all right. Ashley was a welcome sight at the track for so many people who were praying for Tammy. I realized that while I felt I needed to be back at the hospital with Tammy, Ashley needed a little break from what was going on back at St. Joe's. Going to Bristol was a good thing for us both.

On the flight to Ypsilanti, I closed my eyes and started to think about what was happening. I put myself on autopilot and gave in to the moment. I thought about that one flight home, the one I took right before Tammy told me about the cancer. How I hadn't a clue about who she really was and how much she meant to me—even after all our years of marriage. I was happy that this flight was different. This time, I knew. I got it. Love makes the 10,080 minutes in a week worth living. Seven days, straight-up, are ours for the taking.

## MONDAY, JUNE 17

We knew what was happening. Tammy was now in a coma. Tammy's sister Teri came up the night before so Tammy had a full house of family and friends.

Tammy's parents and her brother and his wife headed back to Ohio early that morning. They were exhausted; they had gone days without sleep. There wasn't much to say before they all left. Really, they had said it all over a lifetime of being a family. Tammy would never leave their hearts. They took that promise with them as the doors to their car sliced hard through the air, the ignition woke up the engine, and they drove away.

Early in the afternoon, Connie's girlfriend, Holly sent me a text saying: Connie said Tammy's not doing well, what can I do?

It's a fact: I NEVER ASK FOR ANYTHING from others. But, by now, I had become a pro at doing things I never thought I would do. Yes, there was something. I texted back: *Can you get Connie to come up here and see Tammy?"*

Two seconds later, she texted: *We are on our way.*

I was holding Tammy's hand and telling her everything was going to be all right when Connie walked in. He walked right up to her and stood there and said, "Hey, Tammy, it's Connie." Now, when Connie comes into a room—any room—people click their heels and jump to attention and I swear I felt Tammy's hand flinch. Then, I watched him just talk to her a little bit. Maybe for ten minutes or so. I thanked Connie for coming up and thanked Holly for making it happen. Connie looked at me for a moment longer than necessary, nodded and left. Connie is an amazing human being and what he did in those ten minutes meant more to me than anything he has ever done for me, and trust me . . . that is saying a lot!

I put my hand in Tammy's and held the pair of them to my cheek, my elbows rested in a wrinkle of the beige blanket covering her. I leaned forward.

"Well, you never got to resign," I whispered in her ear.

\*\*\*

Later that afternoon, both Teri and Kim offered to stay the night with Tammy so I could go home and get some much-needed sleep.

For some reason though, I knew that this would be the last night I would ever get to spend with the woman I loved, the woman I married and the woman who I had the most beautiful and amazing daughter with. I wanted to be with my wife for one more night . . . just Tammy and me.

And it was a beautiful night. I dragged the not-so-comfortable recliner over to Tammy's bed and held her hand. I just started talking to her about our life together and how much she meant to me. I kissed her a thousand times. I tried to go back to day one and relive our life together. I apologized for the things I'd done that had upset her over the years. I told her I loved her every chance I could. I told her that I would take care of Ashley and make her proud. I was begging for a miracle at this point . . . hoping like hell she would just wake up out of her coma and say: "Lets go home." I told her that I was the luckiest guy on earth to have such a beautiful and caring wife for twenty years.

That night was our night to say goodbye and nobody else's.

## TUESDAY, JUNE 18

I woke up early the next morning around the time Dr. Craig walked in. He checked the temperature of Tammy's feet and hands. I asked him how much longer Tammy had. He figured maybe a few hours. As he was about to leave, he turned around, his frame filling the door like a linebacker. He said, "This is Tammy, though, and she has proven us wrong so many times before." I nodded my head slowly, hoping he was right. I liked that he recognized Tammy's badass, stubborn side. With nothing left to say, the doctor left.

You could hear the soft hum of machines and people

murmuring at the nurses' station outside our room. Heels clicking against the hard floor trailed off down the hallway. As I was thinking about the doctor's comment, I heard a soft meow come from around the corner. Again, maooooooow.

I'd recognize that thin, high-pitched string of a voice if I was blindfolded in the middle of a desert a thousand miles away from home. Tex was in the building. And he wanted down.

Excuse me, but I can't end it here.

You know where all this is going. You're in the room with me now. Tammy is lying on the bed, her breaths long and soft, people are walking in. I want to take Tammy with us in this last part of our conversation, this exchange you and I have shared on these pages.

I want the story to continue just a little bit longer.

**PART THREE:**

# TRUTH

# INTO THE LIGHT

*"Jim's wife passed today from cancer, prayers sent their way. RIP*
*Tammy O." A post by Fastman-99 on Yellowbullet.com.*
*We all need a pit crew. Sometimes, we even find them in the*
*hearts of strangers.*

Many times, I would pray for Tammy in the quiet little chapel at St. Joe's Hospital while she was recovering from a surgery or getting treatments. I want to go back and remember the feeling of her being close, just a floor away and a few rooms down the hall. This visit today, though, was different. This was the last time Tammy and I would be together.

Plus, Tex was there. I couldn't believe they snuck him in.

Ashley and Teri tumbled into the hospital room carrying what looked like a square box covered by a small blanket. The guilty suspects looked around to make sure the coast was clear, and then unveiled the cream and brown-striped Tabby, named Tex, that had taken over the starring role in our house after Chocolate left us for the big dog park in the sky. Tammy loved that cat and that cat loved Tammy. Ashley took Tex out of his carrier and gently placed him on the bed, where the fur ball snuggled up in the folds of the beige blanket, close to Tammy's side. I wasn't sure if this was one of Teri's harebrained ideas or something Ashley wanted to do. Either way, it wasn't half bad, and I knew Tammy would approve 100 percent. Soon afterward, Jon O's wife Kim arrived, followed by Kathy Kalitta. We began telling stories and cherishing the last few hours with Tammy. Everyone in the room wanted me to tell the story about how

Tammy and I fell in love, so, of course, I did. There was no crying or sadness, just happy memories about a person who had made all our lives phenomenally better.

A little while later, Jon O and my nieces, Jessica and Julia, came in and then both Corey and Colin Kalitta, Scott and Kathy's sons.

To be honest, it felt like a party. Tex purred.

The whole crew was busy celebrating Tammy and talking about how much joy she brought into everyone's lives and throwing the blanket on the cat's head every time one of the nurses came to check Tammy's vitals. We laughed each time the nurses left, like we were getting away with something big. Even in a coma, Tammy seemed to naturally play all of this exactly the way she liked: nobody was paying attention to her, but everyone was together.

Sometime around three o'clock, I was holding Tammy's hand, her palm resting on the titanium wedding band I wore signifying our marriage in Vegas over two decades before. I gently rubbed along the soft lines on her hand. A tissue, balled up at the edge of the side table, fell to the ground. Ashley and the Kalitta boys were giving each other a hard time as usual.

Somewhere in all the noise, my phone vibrated. It was my good friend Randy Green calling to check in on Tammy and to see how Ashley and I were doing. I stepped out of the room and walked down the hallway to talk with him, which was exactly what Tammy wanted. I've heard people say that a person chooses their time to cross over to heaven. It was like Tammy planned for everyone that she loved to be distracted as she took our love all the way to the light . . . all the way . . . into the light.

The light.

At 3:07 p.m., while nobody was paying hardly any attention at all, the line on the monitor went flat. Tammy stopped breathing.

I just finished my conversation with Randy and was walking back to the room when Jon O called me and told me to get back right away. There was something in his voice, a catch, an urgency. Our eyes locked. I bolted down the hallway as fast as I could, in my heart, knowing Tammy was gone. Standing in the doorway of her room, I saw everyone was crying. Tears fell, my shoulders slumped. Gone. I made my way to her side and hugged and kissed Tammy as much as I could. Even though I had known this would be her last day on Earth . . . the line had been crossed now, she wasn't here anymore . . . I wasn't ready to let her go . . . I wasn't ready to live my life without the woman I loved . . . the girl I married . . . the stealer of my heart who had given me, from all that love, a beautiful daughter.

Once I got some control of my emotions, my first solid thought was that Tammy was no longer in pain. She was free. I didn't want to let go of her hand. I breathed in her girly scent. This is it. Once I leave here today, I'm never again going to touch her or be blown away by her sharp, intelligent remarks, or give her a hard time about drinking Mountain Dew, or look into her beautiful green eyes. I gently placed her hand at her side.

The full weight of the moment settled in. Everyone became real quiet.

Click clack. Click clack. Click clack. Louder came the sound. The shiny black shoes of a preacher stood in the doorway, ready to help us in any way he could. Ashley stayed with her mother as the preacher said a prayer for Tammy and the rest of us just outside the room.

Now, with me being Catholic and Tammy being Protestant, our daughter was sometimes left in faith limbo growing up. I wanted her to go with me to the little chapel at St. Joe's after Tammy passed, but she held up her hand and firmly said, "No." She wanted an answer to a question that any daughter who had just lost her mom would ask, "If there's really a God, why did He take Mom? She didn't deserve this."

She was right. Tammy didn't deserve this. But, faith picks up where answers leave off.

I joined Ashley in the hospital room. I was about to take a page from Grandma Hovenac's book. *OK, Grandma, let's see what you've got.* "Look, I'm not the best example of being a religious person or even Catholic," I said, picturing Grandma just rolling her eyes up in heaven and saying "Amen to that." "I do believe. I do believe that God needed your mom for something more important than what she could do down here. Look at us. All that we've gone through helped us become better people and brought us all together and helped make our relationship stronger." *And that made your mother very happy.*

I hugged Ashley before walking back into the hall, feeling very sure about what I'd said.

Just for the record, I love my sister-in-law. And I knew Tammy's passing was a tough hit for Teri as she joined me in the hallway. But, she could be very one-way in her thinking sometimes. People were telling Teri that Tammy was in a better place now, and, of course, that didn't sit well. "If there was a better place, it's with you and Ashley." Teri's desperate voice punched the words something fierce.

The last thing that I wanted to do was rage a religious war with my daughter and sister-in-law. I knew how hard this was on them. I turned to Teri, wondering in the back of my mind, who in the hell was watching the cat, while trying as best I could to give her some peace. She was hurting something fierce. She needed my comfort, not my judgment. "She is in a better place. She's not in pain and she's still with us. She's just not physically here." As I got older, I didn't go to church as much, but I never stopped believing God knew what He was doing. I always thought that the Lord worked in mysterious ways—so mysterious that we're not always meant to understand. Whatever He's got going on with Tammy now, it was important.

And that's how I explained Tammy's journey into the light to my daughter, to my family and to myself. My head lowered. All of a sudden, I felt really tired. That's when, out of the corner of my eye, I saw the blanket-covered carrier covertly getting farther and farther away down the hall.

Tex's big, awesome adventure had come to an end. And, in many ways, mine had too.

## THE NUDIST INCIDENT

*"I didn't want my mom to know I was drag racing for twenty years so I told her I was in prison." – Drag Racer T.C. Lemmons. Humor helps heal even the most bruised of hearts.*

Cowboy Bob. He's like an underwater oxygen tank to a drowning man. Wheels to a teenager. A hundred dollar bill lying on the ground while you're walking the dog. And payday is still a week away. People will tell you he's half crazy, but he's really not.

Ashley, Teri, Cowboy Bob and Jon O's wife Kim and I went to Michigan Memorial Funeral Home to pick out Tammy's final resting place. A really nice lady named Lori, probably in her mid-forties, drove us around the cemetery grounds, showing us potential burial spots and mausoleums. She had dark brown hair, below her shoulders and wore a nice dark skirt with a light top. She wore glasses and when she looked at you, she kind of took you in with full concentration. She never interrupted. In fact, she would always wait a full second before answering your question just to make sure you had completed the thought. She was very polite. The absence of noise in between our exchange of words made the silence deafening. Going to a cemetery is sobering and, without question, we were all sober, which made the excursion that much more serious. Cowboy Bob couldn't take it. I could tell he was mentally winding up for the pitch. Then, the knuckle ball flew.

Since Bob is such a big guy, he sat up front in the passenger's seat while Teri and Kim sat in the middle row of the funeral home-owned minivan, and Ashley and I sat in the very back. Bob looked at

Lori and asked innocently, "Will you guys have plenty of sunscreen?" He even had me hooked at this point. I thought he was turning over a new leaf and crossed my fingers behind my back that his concern for skin protection didn't mean he was giving up drinking.

"Cowboy, I don't understand," said Lori who didn't realize she was being set up for a hit right between the eyes.

"Well, darlin', we're all nudists, and since it's supposed to be hot and sunny next Tuesday, we're gonna need some sunscreen so we don't get a sunburn. We are gonna need some black socks to cover up the men folks' deals too. You got some of those, right?"

We lost it. We roared with laughter. The look on Lori's face was priceless. I almost felt sorry for her. I could see from her eyes going wide what she was envisioning. She couldn't get past the sock. For the rest of us, though, it was like Cowboy Bob had popped a balloon and all that extra air just mixed in with the rest of the world, and together, all of us, the people I was with and all the people at Kalitta and my family and especially Ashley, my beautiful daughter who meant everything to me, would somehow be OK. What better healing mechanism is there in life than laughter?

You've got to know that whatever happens, it's life, and if something like humor can help you turn that corner, take it. At the end of the day, I went up to Cowboy Bob and gave him a big old Texas hug and thanked him.

"You make people feel good about themselves," I said. His reply surprised me.

"Don't you understand?" he said. "That's what you do too, Jim O. For a long time, you've bottled that up. Let it out." Cowboy Bob helped me see that I had changed, that maybe I didn't need to take myself as seriously as I once did.

After Tammy passed, our family and friends kept us moving forward. No sulking. No time to question. I have been fortunate with the people in my life who have helped me find a way through. In return, I tell them that faith and happiness will carry all of us the distance. Honoring Tammy's life means helping others feel good about her going to heaven. That I know for sure.

Grandma Hovenac would have said the same thing.

# A START

*In 1992, Kenny Bernstein was the first driver in NHRA history to top 300 mph. Unlike sports superstars like Bernstein, our really big moments are probably not ever going to be found in the record books.*

I wore my dark black suit with a panda bear tie that Rick Fischer found for me. Getting ready that morning, my fingers fumbled with the top button. It brought me back to my First Holy Communion, putting on that suit, an innocent time. Somehow, I felt like I had come full circle.

I didn't want Tammy to be in a hearse so I hired a horse-drawn carriage. I wanted her to feel like a princess. I think she would have liked that simpler approach. One thing though, she would have been royally pissed about was the fact that there were several hundred people at her service. She always avoided the spotlight being on her. Well, you give a lot of love, you get a lot of love.

I had asked Larry Smiley and his wife Linda—both of whom led many of the Racers for Christ services at the race track over the years, and who had helped me through Scott's passing—to lead Tammy's services. Larry asked if I wanted to give the eulogy, and, of course, I did. I wrote seven pages. I walked through our life together. Turned out to be part story, part confession, part reminiscing. The mood in the room where I was giving the eulogy was comfortable, like worn leather, lived-in and familiar.

In my mind's eye, as I spoke, I could see her. She was in the green dress, walking across the shop with Scott. Then, we were hanging out at the track after a day of racing, my arm around her, my lips on hers. Years flew by and there's that baby girl in our arms. I breathed Tammy's memory in with all my senses and saw that badass wife of mine tearing up Vegas and cheering on the Kalitta team and talking to kids at the track and throwing back the Mountain Dew and dancing the waltz. The problems, the joys, the shortcomings, the years of mistakes and miscommunication, New Year's Eve, our struggle with cancer. I shared all of it with the folks who were nice enough to be with us that day.

Of course, my friend Pat Galvin, lean and weathered and always looking upward with a smile peaking out from under a full moustache, was at the service. A retired racing veteran, he's worked on Funny Cars for Don "The Snake" Prudhomme and Tom "The Mongoose" McEwen as well as for Connie on Scott's Funny Cars back before I became a part of Kalitta Motorsports. I remember fumbling with my phone and texting him the day I found out about Tammy's cancer, that's how close we are.

"It was one of the greatest services," he later said. "It was the only funeral I've ever been to in my life that, just as I think I'm going to lose it, Jim O would say something funny and I would laugh. I couldn't believe it. He went through all the steps of having Ashley and funny times as a family. And then the most remarkable thing happened. Ashley got up and she read about two pages on her mom and her dad and how lucky she was. Now, based on how sick Tammy was over quite a long time, I think that strength came from Jim O and before that the strength came from Tammy."

I thought about that. Ashley's strength came from me. My strength came from Tammy. Yep, full circle of love.

Later, I found this prayer. It made me think of the hills I had climbed with Tammy, with Ashley, and even the ones I climbed alone. Still climb, too. I wanted to share it with you.

*Lord, mighty and holy, but also meek and lowly,*

*You have brought me to the valley of vision—*

*where I live in the depths but see you in the heights,*

*hemmed in by mountains of sin, I see your glory.*

*Help me to learn*

*that the way down is the way up,*

*that to be low is to be high,*

*that the broken heart is the healed heart,*

*that the contrite spirit is the rejoicing spirit,*

*that the repenting soul is the victorious soul,*

*that to have nothing is to possess all,*

*that to bear the cross is to wear the crown,*

*that to give is to receive,*

*that the valley is the place of vision.*

*Lord, in the daytime I can see stars from the deepest wells,*

*and the deeper the wells, the brighter the stars shine;*

*Help me to find your light in my darkness,*

*your life in my death,*

*your joy in my sorrow,*

*your grace in my sin,*

*your riches in my poverty,*

*your glory in my valley.*

Tammy taught me that the opposite of what you think oftentimes is the truth, like it says in the prayer. That from the dark, you can see the light. That many of the things I thought were so important really weren't. That the little things in life are the biggest. It's a start.

# MAN UP . . . YEAH . . . THAT'S WHAT I SAID

*John Speelman's "Blue Bayou" Funny Car was named after his wife's quarter horse. Isn't it a lovely thing when a man can lead with both sentiment and heart?*

What does it mean to be a man?

Put the drum down. We're not chanting around a campfire here. I'm asking the question because if we don't talk about it, we'll never grow as men. For all the women out there reading this book, feel free to take a ringside seat you don't normally get. As you know, men don't talk. The day in sports, items on a honey-do list, the typical go-to question: "How was your day?" and a list of what we did at work pretty much sum up the talking points for millions of men around the world. Wild guess, but I'm just thinking this fact crosses over cultural borders.

When we talk about finding that mosh pit in life, though, that deep well of happiness, how can we not talk about what it means to be a man? On the cover of this book, it says "Life Lessons from a Crew Chief." One of those lessons I learned has everything to do with being a man.

Let me tell you what my answer would have been ten years ago: a man is a guy who wins at everything. On the job. In the gym. In his wallet. Add to that, I would have said, a real man is a winner in other people's eyes. You might say: *I don't feel that way. That's stupid.* So, let's do an experiment. You're walking down the street and you see a guy wearing an Armani suit and shades. He's "the man" right?

Or you watch some hot shot get an award or climb the highest mountain or pump three hundred pounds of iron at the gym or drive away in a Benz or take over a big company and you think: he's "the man." We all do. We're impressed by these things.

Don't feel bad, it's how a lot of people think. It's the way our culture thinks.

What I've learned is that none of those make you a man. Most of those status markers are not even sustainable so if they did make you a man, you'd have to give up the man card the minute you couldn't fit into the Armani suit, pump that iron, afford that Benz or sustain that company. Now, let's bring it to our level—yours and mine—because none of those ritzy things apply to me either. You'd have to give up the man card the minute you lost your job or gained a beer belly or got winded carrying the groceries in the house after waking up from a Saturday afternoon nap. You get the picture.

To showcase some of the lessons I've learned, I asked some of my friends (yep, Cowboy Bob included) to talk about what it means to be a man and how they saw me evolve. I wanted to share a wider perspective on how I got it through my thick skull that I needed to change after Tammy got sick. You're gonna hear some good advice. Even more, you're gonna hear stuff that shows the generous hearts of the people talking.

\*\*\*

Being a man means being a good father, being present.

Jesse once observed that even though I was going through a lot of shit while Tammy was sick, I was a dad first, because I tried to be strong for Ashley. Here's his take: "Not only is Jim O a success story with a championship potential and turning the team around, but, more importantly, he's become a better dad and realized that he has to take care of the stuff that is there and that's that kid. He brought her to the track every weekend and gave her that job doing social media for the team, and she's excelling at it. It has made them a million times closer." *Hey, Jesse, The check is in the mail for the nice comments! You're a great example of being a good father, not to mention the coolest one on the block with all those motorcycles and tattoos!*

Jon O commented on this too. He said: "I didn't like Jim O very much a few years ago. I'm proud of him for the way the cars are running and for his relationship with Ashley." *Thanks, little brother, you always have to lead with a zinger, don't you. Just like when we were kids.*

Part of being a good father, too, is trusting. Tammy taught me that when you love unconditionally, you naturally trust. Being comfortable in my own skin means I trust my decisions and those of others, especially my daughter, who I am so lucky to be around at home and on the job since she joined as Kalitta's social media manager.

Cowboy Bob, the one who had to lay a hammer to my head to make me see how far I'd drifted, pointed out that I could have lost so much more. "Jim O's relationship with his daughter is completely restored. In the end, he not only could have lost his wife but his daughter—emotionally. He didn't because he made it right, he showed her that she mattered. He really found his dick stick." Wow. Thank you, Cowboy Bob.

About fatherhood, there's nobody that brings it home better than my dad. When you get an at-a-boy from the old man, it's big. My dad calls and critiques me every Monday. Oh, my dad was pretty hard growing up. And he should have been. He worked like a dog to support us. Now, he's our biggest critic. But, he's also our biggest fan. He's got everybody's cell phone number. He started texting two or three years ago and now he sends motivational texts to all of us: me, Jon O, Nicky, Del, Tommy D and JR.

Most of those texts you can't repeat. My dad's a real wordsmith. And that's OK because he's there for me. He taught me that being present and responsible, in whatever form these may take, are two of the most important things a father can do. Sacrificing without complaining, selflessness, wanting the best for your kids even if that means moving half way across the country, love without apology . . . these are all qualities in the job description of being a father. Yep, my dad taught me all that. It just took me a long time to appreciate his teaching by example.

***

Being a man means remembering all the reasons you said, "I do."

There are two kinds of guys who cheat in this world. One kind cheats because he wants to have some fun on the side or maybe he thinks there's something better out there. The other kind cheats to get caught. Now, you probably think I'm talking about affairs here, but I'm not. I'm talking about the betrayal in a guy's heart. The kind that creates distance, the kind that makes you stray from the person you vowed to love forever. I was in the second group. I had started to wander from who I used to be, all the while really wanting someone to just say "stop." I did want to be set on the right path but didn't know how to find my way. I had left behind the dorky kid who had strolled into the Little White Chapel and that was a mistake.

Don't ever forget who you were when you first began a life

with someone else.

*\*\**

Being a man means showing up as a leader—at home and at work.

Relationships can be repaired. You can change today, and that's the great part about life. The last six months of Tammy's life on earth was heaven because I finally struck that balance—physically and emotionally—between home and work. I reset my priorities and put myself in the driver's seat. Ashley and I became closer. Our wins on the track improved. It kind of startles me when I think about it. The happier I became at home, the better our team performed. It wasn't coincidence.

Bob Lawson has said that when you're a leader, people see that. As a husband, in the workplace, in life, leading the way and doing the right things matter.

Jesse's right when he says I wasn't the best dad possible. His words helped me to face that truth, and I hope it helps you too. Because forgiving oneself is a big step to moving forward. He says: "Jim O probably wouldn't have made it through the way he did and be the person he is if he didn't have that kid with him every week. That's very important. She wasn't there before. For Jim O, drinking every weekend at races and getting bombed was just a Band-Aid, covering up for some kind of pain. Once you get rid of that, you're forced to say, 'I have to deal with this shit and deal with it and get rid of it.' I drank hard for years for stuff I experienced when I was a kid. Happiness comes when you don't carry a kind of weight and pain that makes you feel guilty . . . forgiving yourself. Maybe for Jim O it was not being the best dad possible. Now, maybe a big part of it is forgiving himself for that and letting go of it." *Jesse, was I that much of a drunk for crying out loud?* Honestly, I know *you are right on all this. The fact that you and others never gave up on me means a lot to me.*

Letting go and knowing what's important, putting the pictures of the people you love squarely in your mind and making sure everything you do is for them, that's what I'm talking about. At the end of the day, being a man means doing what's right for the people you care about. Much later, Jesse told me, "Hey man, you loved Tammy enough to marry her and have a kid. That's the epitome of a man, stepping up and doing what's right and being there for her a million percent. Being there for Ashley. A good percentage of people would be like 'fuck this.' That's a typical reaction, people run away from the fire. But, not you, man. Not you." *You're right, Jesse. It feels good, too.*

So I keep thinking about what made Tammy's last six months so different. I had made the choice that New Year's Eve to strive for something greater in myself. When Tammy and I first started dating, we were true friends from the start. Of course, when you first meet someone, youth kicks in the lust part too. The last six months was different because we were best friends with no conditions, no expectations. We stood by each other. It came from a place deep inside both of us.

A major Kalitta sponsor and die-hard fan, Mac Tools President Brett Shaw put it this way: "If you're going to be married to someone and you're going to have kids, be best friends. Slow down while you're going after your goal. It's about being connected to your team and collaborating with them. When you're the crew chief, you're going to make tough decisions. In a family, you're going to collaborate, too. A true win is when two parties win." *Two parties winning . . . you are spot on, Brett.*

He continues: "I think Jim O learned that near the end, and it's unfortunate that he had to go through something like that . . . being honest, open, proactive, and understanding of the people you're working with—what makes them tick—and trying to help them get to their goals . . . if Jim O can help that team be successful, he will be successful. If you focus on your family, your wife, your kids and they're more important than you, then you will be successful. It's about relationships and family. Jim O's relationship with his team and his family, my gut tells me, it's stronger than it's ever been . . . the focus, the consistency, the desire to win ... flash can be a façade because flash can be fake. There's no flash here." *OK, after hearing all that, I'm still not giving you any points this season for the Ravens. It's Steelers all the way, man! Seriously, thank you, Brett, for recognizing that. I don't deserve your nice words, but I appreciate them.*

I missed out on a lot of moments because of racing and it didn't always put me in the winner's circle at the track or at home. For many years, I didn't realize my biggest support system was my family. If I had seen that sooner, I would have been a different husband, a different father. And I was, the last six months of Tammy's life on earth. I really was.

***

Being a man means having a roadmap.

I think that knowing where you are going and understanding your values are big. It's kind of funny. We spend more time planning a vacation than planning the kind of person we want to be. When it comes to our values and the principles we stand for, I discovered that it's good to really think about them; they are a roadmap to who we are or even the person we might want to become.

Bob Lawson put it this way: "It was a challenging time in their lives when Tammy got sick. It wasn't always roses. Knowing that made me respect Jim O even more for the man he then became. That reminded me of my father when we got the call he had passed away. You either face it and deal with it, or cut and run. Society today cuts and runs a lot. The integrity this place carries is because of the leadership we have, both from Connie and Jim O." *Bob, earning your respect means the world to me.*

A roadmap defines your priorities. Jesse said, "You have to take care of the life you do have. I lost my son I adopted. I went through a horrible divorce four years ago. I have three other kids I have to take care of. Jim O did the same thing. He has to be there for his daughter first and foremost and take care of his responsibility and be the leader of all these guys. Some people would run away and crumble and break down. You have to try to be happy for the time you do have and the things you do have." *Thank you, Jesse, appreciating what you have rather than focusing on what you don't have is probably the best path a man can follow. I've been a lousy example of this for most of my life, but I'm hoping this book will help others see your point.*

Jon O said, "Jim realized what kind of man he was, the gift that God had given him. And he's putting it into play for the right reasons." *You've got it, brother. Thank you for saying something without tacking on an asshole comment at the end for once.*

\* \* \*

Being a man means expanding your man pie.

Call it the man pie. Most men are pretty simple creatures (obviously, this is not in any particular order): We eat. We drink. We conquer battles in our day jobs. We like playing between the sheets. Anything else is gravy. Sometimes, we hit it out of the park by taking the garbage out without being asked or pouring a drink for our wife without her whacking us over the head with the bottle opener. The typical man pie has a few slices and no more. I'd like to think it's because we're deeply focused on doing a few things well. But, that's bullshit. The truth is that we just don't think about much else most of the time.

So, here's a thought. Let's make the man pie bigger. Let's add slices flavored with gratitude and clarity and accountability. Tammy helped me discover these things, and they made me a better man, a happier man.

I'm a lot more grateful because of the many things I've lost; time with someone I truly loved being the biggest loss of all. Being grateful gave me a better attitude at the office, and people have noticed. Being thankful made things in my life better and translated into better relationships, better racing. One of the best parts about putting this into play is taking the time to thank the hell out of others. A lot of guys hate compliments. It's like a compliment cuts them down and makes them feel less of a man. They think: *It's my job. I don't need compliments. What I do is expected.* I felt that way too, like "I'm a crew chief. Don't thank me for it. Don't give me extra points for doing my job." Recognizing people, though, matters. Accepting that recognition matters too.

Pat Galvin was one of the first people to see the change in me. He said I had come through a really dark time and made my life a really bright place. I like how he phrased that. I know for a fact that he doesn't take anything for granted. He's gone through some pretty heavy shit. Whenever he talks to his kids on the phone, he makes it a point to end the conversation by telling them he loves them. "Jim O," he said in his sand gravel voice to me one day, "you're much more in tune with personalities and people now. You're living in the present, not taking anything for granted, but you're thinking steps ahead. Most people don't do that."

Well, I see things I didn't see before. So, I have to ask: Why do we all wait until tragedy strikes before we really appreciate things and people in our life? We sacrifice so much for corporate America and the many "trophies" our culture deems important. Focusing on happiness and life is the opposite of what many of us do. I stopped chasing somebody else's dream, stopped chasing the win. I started attracting happiness by putting all the good things—my wife, our daughter, the people I worked with, the lessons I learned failure—at full throttle.

After Tammy went to heaven, I thought about the opportunities I had to do things differently. If I had admitted my mistakes or walked in her shoes or listened before I talked, I would have been a better person because of it. I hope sharing all this has helped you too.

Because there are still ways to have your pie and eat it too.

You just have to man up and make the damn pie.

# A NOTE TO THE ENEMY

*Unlike many racers who refer to multiple cars by the same name, Arnie "The Farmer" Beswick gave a unique name to each of his cars, including Tameless Tiger, Star of the Circuit, Super Judge and Boss Bird. Cancer doesn't give choices on how you write your script. Someday, though, someday . . .*

Dear Cancer,

Fuck You! You may be the bully on the block right now, but your day is coming when your ass will be kicked!

- Jim O and every single person who has lost someone they loved to cancer and all those who have sacrificed their lives to the merciless, black heart of this fucking awful disease

# BEING A CHAMPION ISN'T WHAT YOU THINK IT IS

*"Not bad for a coupe...." is a quote by "Big Daddy" Don Garlits after watching the first Funny Car in qualifying make a pass, slightly faster than Garlits had just run. Real champions take the losses and move on.*

Sometimes, the biggest champion is not the one smack in the middle of the trophy's circle. Any one of us, no matter who we are, has the potential for greatness.

Tammy was a champion. You could see it in everything she did: the courage to soldier on in the face of cancer, her work ethic and values, her unmatched loyalty to the Kalitta team, the quality she demanded of herself, her humility, her constant vision of the big picture, her ease in putting others first. I took what I learned from Tammy and our life together and brought it to the track.

When you can roll up to the starting line with a 10,000-horsepower Top Fuel dragster and you have 100 percent confidence that the set-up and final tune-up you made is going to help you get every single bit of elapsed time and speed out of that race track, it's a good feeling. Even when you roll up there and you think the car is going to have a great run and it smokes the tires, I still have the confidence in my ability to figure it out. It's all about believing in yourself, believing in your team.

Conventional wisdom says working stiffs like us just want to make more money. But that doesn't build a championship team. Believing in them does. That's why winning doesn't necessarily define a champion. Nope, you've got live it way before you ever get to the track.

\* \* \*

Being a champion means showing you have faith in your team.

The killer air conditions were always tricky in Gainesville, Florida. You were racing at sea level where it's easy to make horsepower (basically this means leaving nothing on the table and going fast as hell!). Combine that with a marginal surface, and it's a tough combo. You have to play to the conditions of the track and adjust. We were able to be greedy in Pomona and Phoenix earlier in the 2014 season because of cool temperatures and awesome race surfaces, but now it was time to race smart. When your car has been running mid to low 3.70s and you've got to be happy running in the low 3.80s, you've got to think your way through. It was no different for our Funny Car teams as they had to figure out how to navigate the tricky conditions and be happy running high 4.0s instead of the low 4.0s and the high 3.90s they had run in Pomona and Phoenix.

Alexis's car made its first run Saturday and blew up at around six hundred feet with smoke and flames coming out from under the carbon fiber Toyota Camry body. She wasn't hurt, thank God. I just knew, though, that Connie would be flaming out upside down. All of a sudden, I see him coming. The nickname "Bounty Hunter" suits him. By definition, a bounty hunter pursues a fugitive, turns him in and receives a reward. Today, that fugitive was Tommy D., Alexis's crew chief and a very good friend of mine, and the consequences would most likely whittle him down to nothin'.

Doug and I walked over to Alexis's pit area, knowing that Connie wouldn't be far behind. We thought we had about ten seconds to figure this out before the Bounty Hunter showed up.

"Hey, what happened?" I said quickly to Tommy D, my heart running fast.

"Oh man. The number five intake adjuster backed out and just jumped out of the cup and blew up," he returned. Tommy was more upset than anyone. I'm sure he felt bad about the potential danger to Alexis. I'm also sure he heard the rumbling of earth with every step Connie took.

"OK," I prepared for the storm. Out of the corner of my eye, I spotted Connie marching toward us. I told Doug, "He's looking for a fight."

If it had been a Vegas bet, I would have scored the jackpot.

Connie screamed in Tommy D's face, "What the fuck happened here?"

"The number five intake adjuster," Tommy said as he prepared for a royal ass chewing, "backed out …"

This wasn't the first problem of the day. Connie was already pissed because his car had shut off from not having any oil pressure. More than that, from day one, he had been very protective of Alexis. He promised Alexis's father John Paul DeJoria, a self-made multibillionaire and founder of Patron Tequila, that he would always put his daughter in the safest and best race car possible, and in Connie's mind, he felt like he went back on his word, which is something he just doesn't do.

"Quit bullshitting me," Connie said, getting redder and redder, his voice a crescendo of sound piercing the air. "I asked you a fucking question about why this fucking car blew up?"

I walked over to where Connie and Tommy D. were standing.

"What is he bullshitting you about?" I said fiercely, like we were WWE wrestlers getting ready to rumble. I had to step in; the slaughter was getting ugly. "He told you the truth."

"Fuck you," he threw my way. Great. By now, it was one big fuck-fest.

"What is the problem? You want to know what the problem is?" he screamed. "There's incompetence going on here!"

"No. There's not," I returned solidly. "This happened and we'll figure out why it happened and we'll fix it." By now, there was a crowd watching the Bounty Hunter filleting his subjects.

"If you want to talk about incompetence, let's take a look at your race car. What happened with that? You've had three attempts at this race track. The first time you had a throttle stop left on after a burnout; the second run, you smoked the tires; and the third run you had to get shut off because you had no oil pressure." My right hand involuntarily rubbed my right eye. It hadn't yet been hit.

I hated what I was doing. I don't like getting mad at a seventy-six-year-old man who I love so much. He doesn't need anger in his life. He's like my dad, and I don't want to fight and scream with him. At the same time, I couldn't let him walk all over everybody and think we were incompetent. Any leader can tell their team they believe in them. A real leader shows it.

"What is your problem?" I continued with as much calm as he had fire. I jabbed the air with my pointer finger right at him. "It seems like the better we do, the more aggravated you get. I don't understand that. I feel like every time we run good, I'm pissing you off. You haven't said shit to me about this year or Doug's car."

"That's not true," the Bounty Hunter said. If it was possible for him to fit one more emotion into the moment, I would have said he was offended.

"I've said it to you," he turned his head to the man standing next to me. "Right, Doug?" Doug nodded yes, desperately hoping that we would both stop arguing with each other.

"Well, you haven't said it to me," I said, keeping my gaze steady on Connie.

"What is your job here?" Connie countered. Oh, playing *thaaaaat card.*

"I take care of Doug's car. I take care of the Funny Cars. I run this business for you. There's nobody in this NHRA pit area who does what I do for you. You don't have incompetent people here. At the end of the day, we're all human. And you should know this being around this sport as long as you have that we all make mistakes. It doesn't make us bad people. I make mistakes every day and I know you do to. If we didn't make mistakes, we wouldn't have things to fix. We go out and we smoke the tires and maybe it's because we pushed the car too hard but we learn from that and it makes us better. There are a lot of positives that came out of today. We learned that our tethering devices work right. We learned that our body latches work right." I had shifted my stance from that of a fighter to a thinker. I thought I saw flashes of understanding in Connie's eyes.

I pointed to Alexis's car and continued. "Look. They're able to run that body again. Look at the problems that the Schumacher Funny Cars have had the last year or so. They go out and blow an engine up and the body disintegrates and shit flies everywhere. We didn't have that problem. Alexis didn't get hurt. Nothing flew in the stands and hurt any of our fans. Even though you don't like the fact that it blew up, there are positives that came out of this that prove what we're doing works."

Now, Connie is the type of guy who can pretty much do and say whatever he wants, and I believe that he has earned that right to do so. He's been racing longer than I've been alive, and he'll always know more about racing, life and business than I'll ever know. But the next words out of his mouth proved why he is so successful in everything he does. He told me that he was sorry that he yelled.

He did not, by any means, have to do that. He could have just stood his ground and we eventually would have moved on, but Connie realized we were going nowhere real fast and it was time to end the petty arguing. Now that's a real man and a real champion!

Somewhere in my long comeback to the Bounty Hunter, I decided it was also time to put the gloves down for good. "I'm sorry, too, Connie. You're like my dad," I said, throwing up my hands. "I love you to death. I'll do anything in the world for you. You know damn well that I'm probably going to end up dying at this place. But we don't need to get so aggravated over things. You've told me before when I've gotten aggravated that I shouldn't get that mad and yell. Here you are doing the same damn thing."

After that, we walked back to his trailer and he showed me why his race car had no oil pressure on the last qualifying run. We went back to racing our cars and working together as a team. He even told a few people that he needed to make some apologies, which he did. It was good.

The next day, Doug won the NHRA Gatornationals. I looked at Connie and said, "Connie, yesterday this time, we were ready to kill each other and, today, we're in love with each other again and sitting in the winner's circle with another Wally."

He goes, "Yep," with that slight shrug and straight, set line of his lips that typically closed a conversation pretty much forever. I chuckled and slapped my hands.

Even though it was hard, standing up for what I believed in was the right thing to do. The day you find it hard to stand up for your team—to fully commit so there are no conflicting agendas on the table—is the day you find out your inner champion has checked out. You're just another solo act trying to make it big.

I always think that things happen for a reason. Maybe we get stronger from bad things or painful things that hurt people we love. Maybe. My argument with Connie was one of the hardest things I've ever done, but it showed my team I had their backs. It showed Connie that I believed in what we were doing as a team. It showed that I believed in what he had taught me for so many years, and that was to believe in yourself and be honest with yourself. That was worth more than any prize we could pocket.

\*\*\*

Being a champion means staying the course with a positive attitude.

There is this quote I read and it goes something like this: "A diamond is just a lump of coal that stuck it out." Well, we're all lumps of coal. It's easy to give up and stay a lump of coal, too. It's not winning that makes a champion, but staying the course. As a leader. As a husband. As a father. As a friend. Quitting, among other demons, is tempting.

The past cannot be undone; it's finished. The future, though, is a wide open road. Someone who helped me see this was Scott Garwood of Transformational Growth Partners, a consulting firm to high performance sports teams. I began working with Scott the summer after Tammy went to heaven. Tall and lanky, balding on top, he carries himself a bit like the Disney character Goofy (without the hat and bad orange turtleneck). His humility, though, is what makes him so approachable and easy to talk to. And he understands champions and how to bring out the best in high performance teams. Working with him and the folks at TGP was like getting a mental tune-up—one you don't read about in most how-to-succeed books. His mantra: Put others first. Put happy first.

Whatever cards you're dealt, you've got to play them with the belief it's going to be great. Trust me, we've seen a lot of shitty stuff on the track—heartache, injuries, even death. Any of those things can take a person down.

But, staying the course with a positive attitude and having your head in the right place paves the way to clinching both kinds of winning—winning races and the real mosh pit kind of happiness. If you set low standards for yourself, you're going to get low standards. If you constantly tell yourself your life is a pile of shit, that's exactly what your life will be: a pile of shit.

For example, last season, we had a meeting about what happened in the pits in Norwalk, Ohio. We had a couple leaks and a few other issues. I took my earplugs out and said, "Let's go over this piece of shit again before we go back out there. I could yell and scream, but that's not productive. I'm just disappointed because I know we can do better so let's work on it and make it better and get it fixed." That was pretty positive compared to the old Jim O.

We had one guy still moping around about it, dragging his lip around. I told him to get over it. When you are in a pressure situation and you fuck up, you have to move on and not worry about it. A lot of people don't realize what goes on in the pits and how much it affects the car's performance. If we don't get the car turned around in time, then we don't race. These guys are athletes; they have to perform. It's better to be a little bit slower and smooth and get it done right than racing through it and having to go back and fix it.

Jesse likens life to a one-lap race where you only get one time around. As he says, "So if you're pissed or resentful or envious or angry or any of those negative feelings, it's like pulling your gear shift back into neutral and not moving forward and not living life to its fullest."

Just ask the Aussie, Bruce Read—my "brother" from Down Under who has a drag racing team of his own. He throws his thick accent around each summer visit. He noticed the air change in our shop: "It's been a lot happier the past two seasons. I've been here when it wasn't a nice place to visit a few years ago. Jim O not only changed the direction of Doug's car, he changed the direction of the entire Kalitta Team. The guys are lifted and it spreads right across. The mood on the shop floor, the mood of the girls in the office ... it started in June 2013. There was sorrow that Tammy was gone, but relief that she was out of pain. Car-wise and team-wise and morale-wise, it's been on the up. The shop in Michigan is all about family." *Bruce, I don't care what you say, I'm still not giving in: American football is better even if you guys think not wearing helmets and pads is cooler. Seriously, it's awesome that you could see how the change in me has impacted our team, brother.*

When I stopped chasing the win, when I let that go, I started enjoying life and seeing it through the eyes of someone who saw the glass as half full. The winning, then, came to me.

***

Being a champion means everyone is on the same pit crew, like a family.

When our race cars started running better, Jon O pointed out how the leadership drives our performance and moves us all forward. He noticed how I understand our race cars better. Because I'm a happier and more confident person, I really focus on wanting to do better rather than feeling like I have to. And even if somebody on the team screws up, I still recognize his or her effort.

I knew I was doing something right when Jon O told me, "At-a-boys are fucking cool." I'm kind of like the ringleader on three of our four cars (Connie's going to do whatever the hell he wants on his car) so we're sharing a lot more and having fun and working together to solve problems.

Results don't lie: the performance in the Funny Car area has definitely gotten better. Both the DHL and Patron Funny Cars finished the 2014 season well, but now it's even better. Why? Because everyone is working together more and that starts with the leadership on down. Camaraderie is a big part of how a car runs— or how any championship team performs. If everybody dislikes each other, the cars are not going to run good. Here's what every high performance team knows to be true: whatever role a person has, it is never just a job because that one person's performance can mean the difference between success and failure for the entire team. In the business world, it can mean the difference between keeping a big client or losing them, finding innovative solutions or accepting mediocrity.

That's one reason we don't have a lot of turnover at Kalitta. When you are all in it together, when you're a family, your team's loyalty jumps off the charts.

And it starts from the top. Bruce Read, in his thick Aussie accent, talked about our pride of work this way: "If the guy at the end of the chain doesn't respect the one above, then what's it all about? The leadership that Jim O provides in the way he runs the car gives Troy Fasching, his assistant crew chief, the leadership to manage his people and his boys marshal behind him. Everything here—from the way Jim O delegates to his leadership style—has influenced the success of the team." *Shit, you're making me feel like I have to buy you dinner next time you're in town, Bruce. OK, I'm kidding. Actually, I really appreciate your words, but we're all in this together—every single person on the Kalitta team. I trust each one with my life. It's all of us or none of us, buddy. You're an honorary member!*

\*\*\*

Being a champion means recognizing your focus—and sharing your passion.

Honestly, I thought he was nuts. The September after Tammy went to heaven, during the U.S. Nationals, Scott Garwood from TGP asked me what I liked to do. I told him I'd always wanted to play Major League Baseball and that I pitched and played third base back before I got a permanent case of the drag racing flu. So, we went to the batting cages. He ducked to clear the cage's entrance. "You let me know," he said with that crazy, goofy grin and smooth voice, "when you connect three times in a row."

I'm tipping and fouling and missing. Finally, I connected three times. He said, "It took you twenty pitches before you hit three solid balls." He counted. I was not impressed.

"What are we doing here?" I asked him with a shrug.

But he had something in his mind, and I could see it just as plainly as I could see the aluminum bat in my hand. He wasn't letting go. "Is there a song that you can listen to that gets you in the zone?"

I sighed. "Kid Rock or, no ...," I stammered, really trying to deliver on a good answer. When I hit a brick wall, I just have to be honest. "I don't understand what you're asking all this for."

"A song," he repeated patiently, "that would relax you and get you focused." I picked a Phil Collins song, "In the Air Tonight," which still centers me today. "Tell me when you're ready. I don't care how many times you listen to it. Then try it again."

I listened to it two times. Within six pitches, I hit the ball three times.

"I'm done here," Scott said.

"What the hell?" *Was I some fucking psychological experiment?* No, I was a guy who had just been shown how to channel his focus. And it continues to work.

It's my go-to song. I sit there and play it on my headphones, sometimes two or three times. When I'm done, I feel better making my final decisions.

When you find your focus, you find your center. And there lies passion. When Connie shares his passion for racing, for example, we all feel it. It's contagious. And when your team feels that same fire you do, watch out because you have the best chance for a holeshot (this is where the strongest of two drivers leaves the starting line first. It's the position you want to be in for whatever job you do).

\* \* \*

Being a champion means having a last-man-standing mentality

ESPN reporter Dave Rieff came over to me once and said, "Don't take any of this the wrong way. I want to find out the difference between Connie Kalitta and Don Schumacher, who's all business and puts a premium on winning. It seems like you and Connie put a premium on family."

I liked the way he phrased that question. Because that's what makes us a championship team no matter what the points say at the end of the season.

Don Schumacher has seven very good teams out there. Seven independently-minded teams that win races and championships. It's hard to argue with what Don's teams have done over the years—they are very good. But we're the Kalitta racing family. We are one team with four cars that believes in the Kalitta way. Without question, everybody comes here to win races and win championships. We want to win as many races and championships as Don's teams have, and we believe we can do that by being who we are.

I used to think there were a lot of differences between Connie and Don. I always knew that Connie had a heart of gold and would do anything for anybody and ask for nothing in return. My opinion of Don was much different than it was of Connie. Yes, I say it "was" different because I have to admit that my opinion has changed a lot recently. Whether it was Don, or the people who work for Don, every Don Schumacher race car at the Epping race in 2013 displayed one of the Tammy O panda decals we made in honor of Tammy. I was very thankful and blown away! Don himself has gone through his own cancer battles recently, and I have found myself talking to him quite a bit about that, along with the topic of racing. I realized that Don is a good guy and someone I enjoy shooting the shit with.

The road to get to where we are as a team today wasn't pretty. Between 2000 and 2006, we won a lot of races and did very well. After that, we struggled and then we lost Scott and struggled through loss and grief. Now, though, we've put all the right people and pieces in place. We are getting closer to competing with those guys for race wins and championships.

I feel good about our team because when you see a Kalitta car in the final-round of a race, you'll see every member of Kalitta Motorsports standing at the starting line. That's why we're different. The camaraderie we have among all four teams is second to none. When Doug wins, everybody wins. When Alexis wins, everybody wins. There is no individual win. That's how we roll. Everyone would run through walls to help each other. There have been many times that one of our teams wouldn't have been able to make the next round if it wasn't for the guys from our other teams pitching in. It's the last-man-standing mentality. Our team is stronger as a unit than any team out there. We don't know any other way. It's the culture we live. It's what Connie wants. It's what I want. My favorite football team, the Pittsburgh Steelers, has a similar philosophy. They've only had three head coaches since 1969. They're stable because they have the right people in place who trust and support each other.

There are many, many times when I take comfort in one simple fact: The people I work with have my back.

\* \* \*

Being a champion means having courage.

There's strength in not letting fear stop you from making a change: Fear of failure. Fear of death. Fear of disappointment. Fear of judgment. When we let fear stand in our way, our wheels get stuck in the mud.

Jesse said that he was proud of how I kept it in drive after Tammy passed. Well, I learned there's a risk in not adapting and not being open to change. It's the same thing with failure. Drag racing is a humbling sport. It brings you to your knees many times during the season. In those instances, courage is what makes you get up one more time. And that's how success trades places with failure.

# 60 SECONDS

*"Big Daddy" Don Garlits gave this advice to young people during an interview with allpar.com: "Do what you love, forget the money, you only pass through here once, enjoy it!" Well said, with one addition: Be with the one you love and show them what they mean to you.*

After Tammy went to heaven, a friend of mine asked me what I would say if she walked into the room and I had one minute with her now. Here's my answer: I'd take up most of that minute telling her how much I love her. Maybe I would tell her I was sorry for the stupid things I did and said. Maybe I would thank her for helping me become a better person. But, most likely I'd probably spend that whole minute telling her I love her.

## WHO TOOK MY MOSH PIT?

*Ernest Hemingway once said: "Auto racing, bull-fighting, and mountain climbing are the only real sports ... all the others are games." Like Hemingway, make clear the things you call your happy place.*

Nobody took your fucking mosh pit. Nobody took mine either. Not even the racers who pick our pockets each time we lose a race. Not even the times we barely make it down the track. The mosh pit is a place we create.

No strings attached.

Stop me if you've heard this one: *I'll be happy when ...*

OK, now, fill in the blank. Except, DON'T FILL IN THE FUCKING BLANK. (I know . . . every hoity-toity doctor of psychology out there who's ever written a book on being happy is going to scratch his or her head and wonder how people like you and I can get away with such "interesting" language. Let them wonder.)

Happiness for me is working my ass off. You think I'm talking just about cars, but I'm not. Happiness is working on my relationship with Ashley, my family, and others. Feeling vested. Yes, Happiness is working on that car, too. When she covers that 1,000-foot race track in 3.7 seconds at over 330 mph, I know every part, every piece, every weld from front to back on that dragster is checked and I feel good about what our team has done. And, sure thing, I like to win. I was born to compete. But it's the road to winning—or losing—that determines happiness. Being happy comes way before you get to the track or pile the kids in the car for a grocery run or walk into the big meeting with the boss or—especially before—you park your car in the garage, walk into the house and see your family after a long day at work.

The mosh pit in life is a place where happiness lives no matter what. It doesn't mean you don't have a bad day. It just means a good day isn't based on material goods or events. For me, understanding this took every part of my life to another level.

For instance, in our first fall season without Tammy, Doug ended a seventy one race winless drought by racing to the Top Fuel victory on Sept. 22, 2013, at the AAA Texas NHRA Fall Nationals at the Texas Motorplex in Ennis. He beat Shawn Langdon whose crew chief is Alan Johnson. It was our first win since Denver; our first win in three years.

Here's the beautiful part. We had a dominant car at the track that day. (Where we won was special, too, since that was the place Tammy said "yes" to being my girlfriend.) Of course, the win was a big deal for us. Even Alan came over and joined in our mosh pit, which meant a lot to me! Reality check, though: Anybody who thinks they can win every race is fooling themselves. There are a lot of people out there with the same goals that I have. That's life too.

Going into that race feeling happy made the whole experience a lot more fun. It was something Scott Garwood and I talked a lot about in the months leading up to that race. Before, I limited myself with being happy only when we won. That fall, I realized that being happy first—before you ever step up to the track—is living a Top Fuel life. Being happy gives you the freedom to have fun and I believe that is what led us to win in Ennis. The epiphany upended the popular paradigm of winning first to be happy.

The approach set our whole team in a forward direction.

Jesse said that you have to take care of yourself in order to take care for your kids or maintain a relationship or achieve success in however you choose to make a living. Not selfishly, where all you worry about is yourself. No, he meant knowing what your happy place feels like and figuring out how to create that life.

After many years and tremendous loss, I finally got it: There are events going on in this world that are way more important than winning a drag race. It is tough to understand sometimes, and I have to work at practicing what I preach. It's not always easy. We are all competitive. But, a drag race is just one part of the day. I get to spend time with Ashley and guys like Connie and Doug and Cowboy Bob, my brother Jon O and all the people at Kalitta who are family to me. I get to tune a 10,000-horsepower nitro burning Top Fuel dragster for a living. That puts me in the winner's circle of life right there.

As I have become a happier person, the cars have begun running better. It's a crazy thing. The workload hasn't changed. The people haven't changed. Being a crew chief means you are responsible for every part of that car and the approach of your driver. Being happy has led to more wins, a better performing team, a better performing car and a better performing driver.

If you're reading this now and feeling like you're not doing the happy dance in your life, don't worry about it. You have time. Time with the people you love, with your work, with your son and your daughter, and your extended family. Hell, every day is just another chance to line up at the track. Just don't put off kicking it into high gear.

For me, that means making good on my promise to Tammy

about Ashley.

While on a trip to Huntington Beach, California, Ashley said, "Hey, Pops, let's go get a couple tattoos."

"We should ask Jesse about it. He'll know where to go," I said, amazed at the two of us and how far we'd come. We were impulsively scheming about tattoos. I loved it.

Ashley texted Jesse and he knew where to go and gave us a number, but since it was a last minute decision, the tattoo artist was on vacation. Eventually, we both did get our tattoos with me getting Ashley's initials and "777" in honor of Tammy's love of slot machines. Recently, I added one with a panda bear playing a slot machine and drinking a Mountain Dew. Long live ink.

Brian Marshall, a partner of Scott at TGP and a great guy who is both wicked smart in business and kind all at the same time, told me that most people learn by first going through a tragedy and then realizing they shouldn't take things for granted. Far more rare is learning from other people's mistakes. When that happens, he calls it "enlightenment." I hope, after reading all this, you will be enlightened by all the mistakes I've made (because I've made enough to go around for everybody).

Oh, and I did promise when we stepped off the starting line that I would take you to the real mosh pit. Stay with me a little longer. We're almost there.

One last thing. If you take away absolutely nothing else from this story, let me leave you with the most important lesson Tammy taught me about happiness: unconditional love. I made a lot of mistakes in my life, but she always loved me no matter what. She could be madder than hell at me and still say those three little words (through clenched teeth, sometimes). I could forget something or overlook something or say something stupid (which happened quite a lot), and she never quit on me. She looked past the flaws and saw me for who I really was deep down, even though it took a long time for that guy to fully surface.

Tammy, above all others, taught me how to live a Top Fuel life.

# LAST RUN

*Funny Car legend Russell James Liberman's nickname was "Jungle Jim." Fans shortened it to just Jungle. Sometimes, what sticks in life is different than what we intended.*

Nothin' beats the full weight of the sun when it starts to rise in the morning. Pretty damn breathtaking. Everything is dark and then, boom, out of nowhere, the sun does a burnout like a Top Fuel dragster, spreading its light in smoky sweeps of orange and pink and violet.

As the light spreads wide, it reveals ordinary objects. Like a pen or a lamp or a book. Routine stuff. Once in awhile, though, you notice things you never saw before in the middle of all that ordinary. A red sailboat in the background of a photo or a letter you had tossed aside. And you wonder, "Why didn't I see that red sailboat before?" or "What made that person write that?" You make these small discoveries and you feel a little different inside, like you found hidden treasure. The details were there all along. You just hadn't seen them.

Life is like that too. If you let in the light, you'll see things as being more significant than you thought. You'll see something for what it is. All these ordinary things become not so ordinary. Happiness. Straight-up.

The real mosh pit.

It was inside you all along.

\*\*\*

When I close my eyes now, I can still smell the fresh, white sheets and chai tea lattes in Tammy's room back at St. Joe's Hospital. I prayed there. I want to go back to that little chapel at St. Joe's and say a prayer for her again soon. I know God needed her for something greater in heaven, something greater than what she could do here. I know she's made heaven an even better place.

Lucky for me, I talk to her all the time. I ramble on. And on. Every time I see Tammy at the cemetery, I tell her all sorts of shit, both good and bad. (When I die, she's probably going to kill me again for all the dumb shit I continue to do and probably won't quit doing anytime soon.) But the great part is that I don't ever have to wait to tell her—or even write a letter to her—about how much I love her or that I miss her every day or how the team is doing.

She already knows.

# Acknowledgments:

All the Fans of NHRA Drag Racing . . . without you, there's no racing and no story.

Wally Parks . . . for starting the NHRA.

Graham Light . . . my go-to guy at NHRA and my friend.

Every racer no matter what form of motorsport you're in.

Every Crew Chief I compete against . . . your dedication and passion for the sport of drag racing pushes me to work hard each and every day.

The PRO Board . . . for allowing me to be on the Board of PRO and working towards building a positive future for all drag racers.

Every Sponsor we have ever had at Kalitta Motorsports . . . I have learned so much from each and every one of you. Without you . . . Kalitta Motorsports is not what it is today.

Dave Rieff, Mike Dunn and the entire ESPN NHRA Broadcasting Team . . . You all have been there for us through good times and bad.

All of the Doctors, Nurses and Volunteers at St. Joe's Hospital . . . thank you for your support of Tammy through her battle with cancer.

Racers for Christ, Larry and Linda Smiley . . . thank you for being there for me so many times.

Everyone I ever worked with at Kalitta Motorsports both past and present.

Every Teacher I ever had . . . even though it appeared that I wasn't paying attention, I really did learn something from all of you, and for that I thank you.

Greektown Casino and The Fullhouse Restaurant . . . two of Tammy's favorite places.

Scott Garwood and Brian Marshall . . . for pushing me to write this book and thinking my story will make an impact.

Michele Kelly . . . for guiding me through this book writing process and allowing me to curse in it.

Everyone at JJR Marketing, for believing in my story.

Every Kickstarter Supporter . . . your generosity was amazing and I thank you all for making this book a reality! You guys and gals are badass!

Steve Randall, Randy Weldon, Sylvia McCormick, My Friend "Big" Brad Fornes, Russell M. Moon, Brian K. Lanfear, Jim Parks #Team DHR, James Oldfield and Duane Shields…this is my Kickstarter Acknowledgement Crew, and I want to thank each one of them for their support of this book.

John Aden . . . for believing in myself and the Kalitta Team when this Mac Tools program first got off the ground.

Tony Merritt . . . you never gave up on the Mac Tools/Kalitta partnership, plus you made Tammy and Teri blush.

Roger Spee . . . yeah yeah yeah!

Brett Shaw . . . your professionalism and passion about Mac Tools and Kalitta Motorsports has taken our partnership to a whole other level

The Poulin family . . . you are family!

Reg Kenney . . . your passion about the Kalitta Team is amazing.

Cameron Evans, Tim Kerrigan and Red Line Oil . . . your support of the Kalitta Team and me through thick and thin.

Ed Justice Jr. and Justice Brothers . . . an amazing man and an amazing company.

John Paul DeJoria . . . you are truly a motivating human that I am proud to know.

Jim Read and Santo Rapisarda Racing . . . you both brought me and my family to Australia to race and experience your country, and for that I thank you both!

All the Australian drag race fans.

Frank Johdus and Jim Grace . . . for partnering with my dad and running the Pleasure Seekers Top Fuel Dragster.

Hank Endres, Chip Brown and Bill Clark . . . for allowing my dad to join the Nirvana Top Fuel Team when the Pleasure Seekers Team quit racing.

Frank Cook, Big Chuck, Tuna and Morris McDonald . . . for letting me tag along with you guys on the Drag On Charger Alcohol Funny Car.

Jay Meyer...for allowing me to work on your Alcohol Dragster and teaching me so much about racing.

Allen Hawkins . . . for being my friend way back when we were kids, and still being my friend today.

Randy Green . . . for being my friend and teaching me so much in my early years of drag racing

Fraternal Union of Crew Members . . . enough said.

The Pittsburgh Steelers and the Rooney Family . . . watching and cheering for your organization for all of these years taught me a lot about loyalty and respect.

Ken and Judy Black . . . you both are beautiful people with huge hearts.

Kenny Bernstein and Don Prudhomme . . . for setting the standard on professionalism in drag racing.

Trish Stuckey, Ashleigh Alarcon and all of my dance friends . . . for teaching me that ballroom dancing is fun.

Maynard Ynigst . . . you were the first one who believed I could make it as a crew chief someday.

Frank Bradley . . . you taught me so much in a short amount of time and continue to be my friend.

Jim Becker . . . I learned so much about engines and machining from you.

Dick LaHaie . . . I am not what I am today without your mentoring, and pushing me to be the absolute best I can be. You are the best Dick O!

Ed "The Ace" McCulloch . . . you allowed me to take the next step in racing and continue to be a hero and a close friend of mine.

Nicky Boninfante, Donnie Bender, Doug Dragoo and Jon O . . . the best bunch of championship winning misfits I ever worked with.

 Tim Richards . . . you taught me that Connie and I are good working together, and you helped me figure problems out when you didn't have to.

Alan Johnson . . . you have helped and taught me so much in so many ways over the years.

Jimmy Prock . . . for teaching me that hard work will get you somewhere in life.

Melodie Martin-Angelo . . .Tammy just loved you!

Johnny D . . . Outstanding!

Bruce Read . . . you are my Aussie brother.

Rick Fischer . . . you can be a pain in the ass, but I love ya.

Ashley Cugno . . . for the new experiences in my life.

Uncle Ray and Aunt Marie . . . for being awesome and being family, and when I made the move to Michigan, you made sure that I knew I had family there, which made this big move seem not so big.

Aunt Vickie and Uncle Bob . . . for simply being you and being there for me at all times from the day I was born.

Aunt Bettie and Uncle Richie . . . for being some of my biggest fans and being family.

All of my Aunts and Uncles and their families.

All of my cousins and their families.

Grandma and Grandpa "O" . . . I love and miss you both.

Grandma and Grandpa Hovenac . . . the love you showed me growing up is second to none! I was honored to be your first grandchild.

Bigger Grandma . . . you were simply the most badass great grandma ever.

Isaac Mallett . . . for caring and loving my daughter. You couldn't have come along at a better time for Ashley. I know Tammy would have loved you.

Jesse James . . . you tell it like it is, and for that I thank you.

Alexis DeJoria . . . you can do anything in the world that you want, but you chose to be part of the Kalitta Family, and for that I am grateful.

Del Worsham, JR Todd, Chad Head and Brandon Bernstein . . . pure badasses behind the wheel, and great friends as well.

Hillary Will . . . for always giving 110% while you were my driver.

David Grubnic . . . for helping make the Kalitta Team better and being a chauffeur for Tammy, Ashley and I down in Australia! Good times!

Troy Fasching and Mac Savage . . . without you two, I would be lost.

My Mac Tools Crew . . . you guys are awesome.

The Kalitta Motorsports Office Girls: Patricia Nielsen, Shawn LaJoice, Sarah Rauen, Megan Korican and Chrissy Danowski . . . you have helped Tammy, Ashley and myself in so many ways. Tammy loved you all!

Nicky and Rob Boninfante . . . for simply being my brothers from another other mother.

Tommy DeLago . . . for coming back home and making our Kalitta Team even stronger.

Rachel DeLago . . . for being my friend and always caring and being there for Ashley when she needs a big sister. Go Blue!

Bob Lawson . . . we have been through a lot together my brother!

Sarah Ryan . . . you came into my life at the right time and allow me to be me, which is scary!

Pat Galvin . . . you are truly a friend and someone who I can always count on.

Nick Galvin . . . your positive attitude about everything you're involved in is amazing! You are my buddy!

George Henderson . . . your advice when I first came to work for the Kalitta's is something that I'll never forget.

Flapping Bob . . . for your friendship for so many years.

Donnie Couch . . . for making my sides hurt from laughing at all of your bullshit.

The Bakersfield Hospitality Crew . . . for giving me a place to hang out and talk with my heros of drag racing.

The entire Ferrell and Matoski families.

Tim and Therese Ferrell . . . for being there when you were needed most.

Teri and Bubba Sewell . . . for being my goofy sister-in-law and one of my early heros of drag racing.

Keith and Virginia Ferrell . . . for having the most amazing and beautiful daughter in Tammy.

All of my nieces and nephews . . . Jess, Julia, Ryan, Jared, Samantha and Joseph.

Suzie O . . . for simply being my sister with an amazing voice and I love you!

Mace Maben . . . you rock, brother-in-law.

Kim Oberhofer . . . for being there for Tammy so many times, and being my sister in-law.

Jon O . . . I am proud to be your big brother and proud of the father and husband that you are! I love you, brother!

Mom and Dad . . . for being my mom and dad and providing for me as a kid! I love you both!

Doug Kalitta . . . for being like a brother to me and one badass race car driver. I hope we can win a championship together before we are all done.

Kathy Kalitta-Hindman . . . for being there for Tammy and being there for me. You kick ass!

Corey and Colin Kalitta…you two remind me so much of your dad and he would be so proud of you both.

Scott Kalitta . . . for taking a chance on me and being my mentor and big brother. You always listened to me and told me how it was. I miss you!

Connie Kalitta . . . you are like another father to me and you and your family mean so much to me. You have taught me so much about racing, business and life. Thank you for coming to see Tammy before she passed…you meant the world to her and she loved you very much!

Cowboy Bob . . . you are the older brother I never had and my best friend. When I need to be straightened out . . . you straighten me out. When I need someone to talk to . . . you listen. I love you, bro!

Chocolate and Tex . . . two amazing pets that Tammy loved very much. You both meant so much to Tammy and brought so much joy and happiness to her.

Ashley Oberhofer . . . you are everything to me! You remind me so much of your mother, and I couldn't be prouder of you, and I know your mother would be equally as proud. I love you more than life itself, sweetie!

Tammy Oberhofer . . . you were my wife, my true love and my best friend. You loved me unconditionally when I didn't deserve your love. You were an amazing mother and wife and the most courageous person I know. I miss you so much and I love you even more!

*Everyone who I may have forgotten . . . I'm getting old and I have that CRS Syndrome, which means "Can't Remember Shit."*

# Special Dedications:

To Katherine, Patrick and Peter Kelly, my three "everythings."
Love, **Mom**

In Loving Memory of Louise E. (Markham) Papallo 1951-2012
**- The Papallo Family**

To Fish and Rita Garwood whose dedication to family have made their children the adults they are today. We miss you both and will strive daily to make you proud of us.
**- The Garwood Kids**

Jim O:
I am excited for your book launch and hope your story helps any one who may be facing challenges in life by giving them the opportunity to reflect on how you and Ashley O have been able to deal with Tammy's passing. I'll never forget how strong you and Ashley were during Tammy's funeral and I am very thankful to have you both and Tammy's memory in my life. Good luck and thank you for sharing your life with others. God Bless.
**- Bob**

Jeannine,
You are the best crew chief we could ever have!
Love always.
#KalittaStrong
**- Katie, Bennett, and Scott**

Living in the dash with my wonderful wife Gina.
**- Tom Land**

# The Making Of This Book

The cover photo depicts crew chief Jim Oberhofer at a race during the 2013 NHRA season. The font used for headlines in *Top Fuel for Life* is *Bebas* and *Trade Gothic Bold*, chosen for their bold strength and weighty character. The book's designer Juan Pablo Ruiz chose *Adobe Caslon Pro* for body text because it is "just a good classy body font for books." The NHRA Communications Department Style Guide served as reference for racing-related terms. All other phrasing was referenced using *The Chicago Manual of Style*, 16th Edition. The dictionary of choice was *Merriam-Webster*.